P9-DBV-802

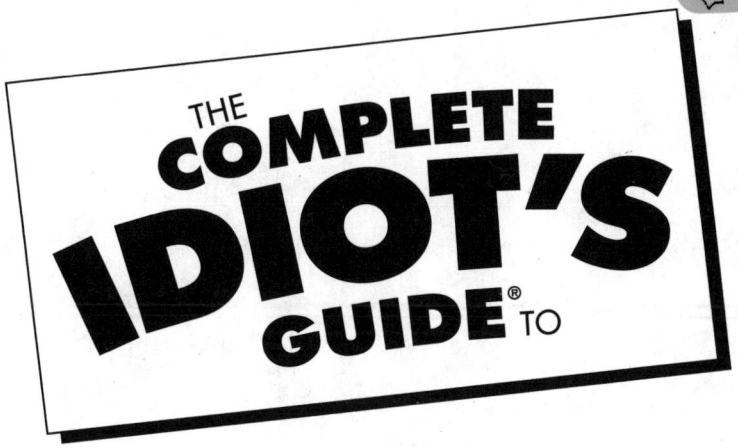

U.S. History, Graphic Illustrated

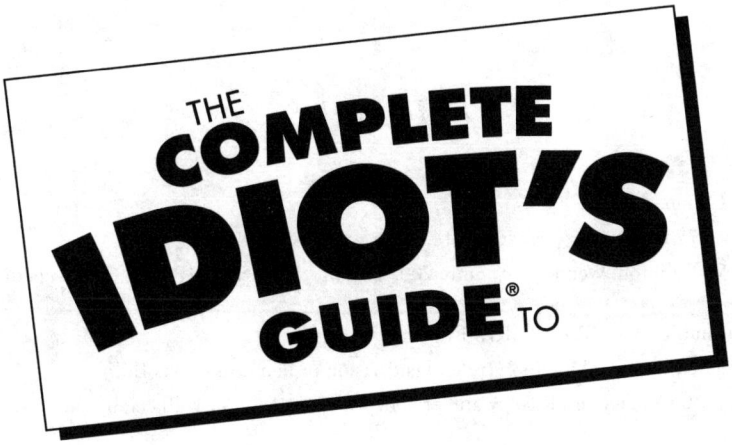

U.S. History, Graphic Illustrated

by Kenneth Hite
Illustrations by Shepherd Hendrix

A member of Penguin Group (USA) Inc.

For Harold Hite

ALPHA BOOKS

Published by the Penguin Group

Penguin Group (USA) Inc., 375 Hudson Street, New York, New York 10014, USA

Penguin Group (Canada), 90 Eglinton Avenue East, Suite 700, Toronto, Ontario M4P 2Y3, Canada (a division of Pearson Penguin Canada Inc.)

Penguin Books Ltd., 80 Strand, London WC2R 0RL, England

Penguin Ireland, 25 St. Stephen's Green, Dublin 2, Ireland (a division of Penguin Books Ltd.)

Penguin Group (Australia), 250 Camberwell Road, Camberwell, Victoria 3124, Australia (a division of Pearson Australia Group Pty. Ltd.)

Penguin Books India Pvt. Ltd., 11 Community Centre, Panchsheel Park, New Delhi—110 017, India

Penguin Group (NZ), 67 Apollo Drive, Rosedale, North Shore, Auckland 1311, New Zealand (a division of Pearson New Zealand Ltd.)

Penguin Books (South Africa) (Pty.) Ltd., 24 Sturdee Avenue, Rosebank, Johannesburg 2196, South Africa

Penguin Books Ltd., Registered Offices: 80 Strand, London WC2R 0RL, England

Text Copyright © 2009 by Idea & Design Works, LLC
Illustrations Copyright © 2009 by Shepherd Hendrix

All rights reserved. No part of this book shall be reproduced, stored in a retrieval system, or transmitted by any means, electronic, mechanical, photocopying, recording, or otherwise, without written permission from the publisher. No patent liability is assumed with respect to the use of the information contained herein. Although every precaution has been taken in the preparation of this book, the publisher and author assume no responsibility for errors or omissions. Neither is any liability assumed for damages resulting from the use of information contained herein. For information, address Alpha Books, 800 East 96th Street, Indianapolis, IN 46240.

THE COMPLETE IDIOT'S GUIDE TO and Design are registered trademarks of Penguin Group (USA) Inc.

International Standard Book Number: 978-1-59257-785-9
Library of Congress Catalog Card Number: 2008920996

11 10 09 8 7 6 5 4 3 2 1

Interpretation of the printing code: The rightmost number of the first series of numbers is the year of the book's printing; the rightmost number of the second series of numbers is the number of the book's printing. For example, a printing code of 09-1 shows that the first printing occurred in 2009.

Printed in the United States of America

Note: This publication contains the opinions and ideas of its author. It is intended to provide helpful and informative material on the subject matter covered. It is sold with the understanding that the author and publisher are not engaged in rendering professional services in the book. If the reader requires personal assistance or advice, a competent professional should be consulted.

The author and publisher specifically disclaim any responsibility for any liability, loss, or risk, personal or otherwise, which is incurred as a consequence, directly or indirectly, of the use and application of any of the contents of this book.

Most Alpha books are available at special quantity discounts for bulk purchases for sales promotions, premiums, fund-raising, or educational use. Special books, or book excerpts, can also be created to fit specific needs.

For details, write: Special Markets, Alpha Books, 375 Hudson Street, New York, NY 10014.

Publisher: *Marie Butler-Knight*
Editorial Director: *Mike Sanders*
Senior Managing Editor: *Billy Fields*
Acquisitions Editor: *Karyn Gerhard*
Senior Development Editor: *Phil Kitchel*
Senior Production Editor: *Megan Douglass*

Cover/Book Designer: *Bill Thomas*
Indexer: *Brad Herriman*
Layout: *Brian Massey*
Proofreader: *John Etchison*

Contents

Part One: **When in the Course of Human Events 1775–1815** 2

In which we fight the American Revolution (and the French and Indians), overthrow tyranny, avoid dictatorship, keep slavery, experiment with Articles of Confederation, and write the Constitution. Then we elect George Washington. After that, we fight our first cliffhanger election, the Barbary pirates, and the British (and the Indians) again.

Part Two: **A House Divided 1815–1865** 42

In which we try to compromise with ourselves and fail. We invent baseball and American literature, and remember the Alamo. We fight more Indians (and fail the ones we don't fight) and Mexico, expand the West (and slavery), rush to California, get churched up and Transcendental. Then we kill over 600,000 Americans in the Civil War—including Abraham Lincoln.

Part Three: **Yearning to Breathe Free 1865–1898** 72

In which we rebuild, regroup, and resume what we were doing before we so rudely interrupted ourselves. We free the slaves, but not much more. We finish off the frontier (and the Indians) and pick up Alaska and Hawaii. We go on strike, join a union, and turn on the lights. We make billionaires and railroads and the City Beautiful. We get churched up and populist.

Part Four: **Rendezvous with Destiny 1898–1945** 98

In which we go overseas and fight the Spanish, and the Filipinos, and the Germans (twice), and the Japanese. Black folks get the blues and go North, white folks get Progressive and go for two Roosevelts, women get the vote, and everybody gets a Ford. We invent jazz, radio, movies, and comic books, and we keep on inventing American literature (mostly in Paris, 'cause it's cheaper). We get the flu and Prohibition and the Bomb.

Part Five: **Tear Down This Wall** 132

In which Martin Luther King has a dream, and tears down a wall; the revolution is televised. Also, we fight North Korea (and China) and North Vietnam and Iraq (twice), and Communism until the Soviets tear down their Wall, too. We lose two towers, but we get the Moon and the Internet and the Green Revolution.

Index 186

Foreword

Some of the folks who bought this book have skipped right over this foreword and gone on to the good stuff. Good for them, but it's of no use talking to them here.

Some of you are reading this foreword because you figure you're supposed to. You've paid for the book, it's part of the book, so you'd better take it in. To those people, I say skip it. The pictures are just a couple of pages away. A rebellion is about to start. Ben Franklin, Tecumseh, Booker T. Washington, and Edith Wilson await. Get going!

But there are some of you who are reading this foreword because you're looking for reassurance. You have your doubts. You want to read up on American history, but this? This is a big, thick comic book. Is that really appropriate? Is it respectful? Isn't history supposed to be a recitation of names, dates, and things that happened?

No. History is people. History is people doing things, and having things done to them by other people. It is stories, and it is very human stories. The names, the dates, the events are part of it, but you'll miss the story if you just look at the dry recitation. On every page of this tale there are people, brought to delightful life by the masterful pen of Shepherd Hendrix. The characters here don't each get much space, as there is a cast of hundreds and time must fly by at more than a year per page. But in a glance, each figure is made wholly human in a way that a short spurt of text or reproduction of a staid official portrait could not match. The book is informative and honest without being stilted. Kenneth Hite's script brings you the facts, but is not bereft of a point of view, nor a sense of humor.

And while you're zooming your way through over two hundred years of America, pause a moment to consider the art form in which you're reading it. Each moment is immediately brought to life, each character has a face, each event has a visible setting. The comics form makes it all comprehensible. It's not that comics are unique in this. You could make a film covering the very same content you see here. With the hundreds of locations and the hundreds of speaking rolls, such a film would not only be quite costly, it would also require the cooperation of an army of camera operators, lighting technicians, sound designers, location scouts, craft service providers, personal assistants, best boys, key grips, dolly grips, and other folks handling the most minute of efforts. This book, on the other hand, is (despite the help of a few editors and paste-up people and one foreword writer) the clear, undiluted effort of two creative souls. They bring their tone and their vision to the page without tripping over the well-meaning intent and cooperative attempts of so many others.

Comics, as a form, is thriving in an ever-growing array of uses. Like the American colonies themselves, the comics medium operated for a long time limited by the assumptions of outsiders as to what it was supposed to be. And like those colonies, once it freed itself from the limitation of those assumptions, it proved itself capable of achievement far beyond what anyone foresaw.

But forgive this fervent comics booster his digression. A story awaits you! It starts with a gunshot, ends with a victory, and in between you will find struggle, tragedy, betrayal, discovery, conflict, and wrong paths taken. Good intents will go astray, great things will be built on flawed foundations, frailties will bring down the powerful.

So turn the page. The shot is about to fired ....

—Nat Gertler
February, 2009
Which will be history by the time you read this.

Introduction

Regardless of what you may have decided in high school, there is no such thing as boring history. There are, however, an awful lot of boring historians, and an awful lot more boring history books. My great design, my big plan, my desperate hope is that *The Complete Idiot's Guide to U.S. History, Graphic Illustrated* is not one of them.

I have some aces up my sleeve here, of course. First, it's "graphically illustrated"—or as we used to say in the historical United States, it's a comic book. The comic book is an American invention, after all—an American art form, an American way to tell stories. (Yes, there were "picture-stories" in Europe before *The Yellow Kid* became the first successful American comic strip. Like millions of other Europeans, comics had to move to America to get big and successful.) Something about the always-moving rhythms of the set-up and punch line, the friendly conversation between picture and words, just *works* for American speech and story.

Second, I had the advantage of limited space. The book had to cover everything from Lexington Green in 1776 to Grant Park in 2008 in less than 200 pages, and it had to at least mention all the presidents, most of the wars, and the rest of the historical highlights. That meant I just couldn't waste any time or space boring the reader. There just wasn't room! There was always another election, or a wonderful invention, or some new upheaval to discuss on the next page—or the next panel.

In between battles and legislation, I stuck in the things we consider American—hot dogs, baseball, cowboys … and comic books. (And the things we Americans need to remember, but maybe don't want to—slavery, what happened to the Indians, riots, and James Buchanan.) Economics, the arts, industry—the American versions of all those things deserved coverage where I could find it. A few big stories demanded to be woven through the whole book: the African-American experience, the West, religion, immigration. Giving those stories some space helped, again, to keep the book from slowing down too much in any one spot.

My last big advantage, of course, is that while there is no such thing as boring history, some histories are way better than others. I got to write about the history of the United States, which—well, I'll let the least-boring American historian ever, Bernard DeVoto, tell it:

> *Sure you're romantic about American history … it is the most romantic of all histories. It began in myth and has developed through centuries of fairy stories. Whatever the time is in America it is always, at every moment, the mad and wayward hour. … If the mad, impossible voyage of Columbus or Cartier or La Salle or Coronado or John Ledyard is not romantic, if the stars did not dance in the sky when the Constitutional Convention met, if Atlantis has any landscape stranger or the other side of the moon any lights or colors or shapes more unearthly than the customary homespun of Lincoln or the morning coat of Jackson, well, I don't know what romance is. Ours is a story mad with the impossible, it is by chaos out of dream. It began as dream and it has continued as dream down to the last headline you read in a newspaper, and of our dreams there are two things above all others to be said, that only madmen could have dreamed them or would have dared to—and that we have shown a considerable faculty for making them come true.*

I just had to expand that out to fill 176 pages, and I didn't even have to draw any of it. I hope you enjoy the result. I don't think you'll be bored, at least.

Kenneth Hite
Chicago, 2009

Trademarks

All terms mentioned in this book that are known to be or are suspected of being trademarks or service marks have been appropriately capitalized. Alpha Books and Penguin Group (USA) Inc. cannot attest to the accuracy of this information. Use of a term in this book should not be regarded as affecting the validity of any trademark or service mark.

PART ONE

WHEN IN THE COURSE OF HUMAN EVENTS

1775-1815

BANG
April 19, 1775. Lexington Green.
It was "the shot heard 'round the world."
And nobody knows who fired it.

The British (and some Americans) say it was a local yokel hiding in a bar.
The Americans (and some British) say it was a British officer trying to "disperse the damn'd rebels."
BLAM
AAA
And some historians think it just sort of … happened.
Just like the whole American Revolution. The British (and some Americans) said the rebels were a bunch of wealthy, spoiled ingrates who just wanted to get richer.
The Americans (and some British) said the British were rapacious thugs trying to impose tyrannical rule.
WAR!
But most folks thought it just sort of … happened.

After all, 20 years before, Britain and its American colonies had had a common enemy: the French!
CANADA
The French and British both claimed the Ohio Valley, rich in furs and tempting for farmers.
IT'S MINE!
C'EST LA MIEN!
THIS CAN'T END WELL.
In 1754, Governor Dinwiddie of Virginia sent a 22-year-old militia colonel to enforce the British claim.
He stumbled over a French patrol, and …
IT JUST SORT OF … HAPPENED.
… started a world war.
In America, it was called the "French and Indian War" …
KNOW THY ENEMY
… and the French and Indians lost.

WITH THE WAR OVER, THERE'S SOME GOOD NEWS AND SOME BAD NEWS. THE GOOD NEWS IS WE'RE CUTTING THE TAX ON SUGAR.
THAT'S GREAT, BUT WE NEVER ACTUALLY PAID THAT TAX.
WELL, CASH IS KIND OF TIGHT ... I SUPPOSE I CAN PAY IN COLONIAL PAPER MONEY...
WHAT? OUTRAGEOUS! I'LL WRITE A PAMPHLET DENOUNCING IT!
THAT'S FINE, AS LONG AS YOU BUY A STAMP FOR IT.
THE TAX STAMP YOU NEED TO HAVE ON ANYTHING YOU PRINT FROM NOW ON.
AND WHAT, EXACTLY, ARE ALL THESE TAXES BUYING ME?
THE BAD NEWS IS WE'RE ACTUALLY COLLECTING IT NOW.
AHH, WE'RE MAKING YOUR PAPER MONEY ILLEGAL, TOO.
WHAT STAMP?
BRITISH SOLDIERS!
BUT THE FRENCH ARE GONE! WE DON'T NEED BRITISH SOLDIERS!
EXCEPT THE ONES WE'RE GOING TO QUARTER IN YOUR HOUSE, OF COURSE.
To protest the Stamp Act and the rest of these new laws, the colonists sent a high-powered lobbyist to London: Benjamin Franklin.
THEY WON'T BE ANY TROUBLE. YOU'LL NEVER NOTICE THEY'RE THERE.
He was an internationally famous scientist ...
I'M GOING TO HAVE TO SAVE A LOT MORE PENNIES.
A talented inventor ... and, perhaps most important ...
A prolific printer, newspaperman, and pamphleteer.

I HAVE GOOD NEWS AND BAD NEWS. THE GOOD NEWS IS THAT PARLIAMENT HAS REPEALED THE *STAMP TAX* ...
HURRAH!
... AND IMPOSED NEW TAXES ON LEAD, PAINT, OIL, GLASS, PAPER, AND TEA.
IT'S ENOUGH TO MAKE AN *HONEST MAN* TURN TO SMUGGLING.
IT'S ENOUGH TO MAKE A *PATRIOT* STOP BUYING BRITISH GOODS.
SMUGGLING? BOYCOTTS? IT'S ENOUGH TO MAKE A *KING* SEND SOME SOLDIERS TO STRAIGHTEN THIS RABBLE OUT!
On March 5, 1770, British soldiers fired on a protesting crowd – or an angry mob – in Boston.
IT'S ... IT'S A *BOSTON MASSACRE!*
WELL, LEGALLY, IT'S A *BOSTON MANSLAUGHTER.* OR EVEN A *BOSTON JUSTIFIABLE HOMICIDE.*
Rabble-rousing patriot Sam Adams wanted to use the incident to inflame the colonies. His lawyer cousin John Adams wanted to avoid inflaming the British with a lynching.
ALL RIGHT, WE'RE REPEALING ALL THE TAXES, EXCEPT THE ONE ON TEA.
I DON'T CARE. I DON'T DRINK YOUR FILTHY TAXED TEA. I DRINK *BALSAMIC HYPERION.*
WHAT'S IN THAT?
SMUGGLED TEA, MOSTLY.
Tea smuggling was ruining the British East India Company. In 1773, Parliament passed the Tea Act, allowing the Company to dump its tea in America at rock-bottom prices.
TEA
TEA
In response, Sam Adams and his "Sons of Liberty" dumped Company tea in Boston Harbor.

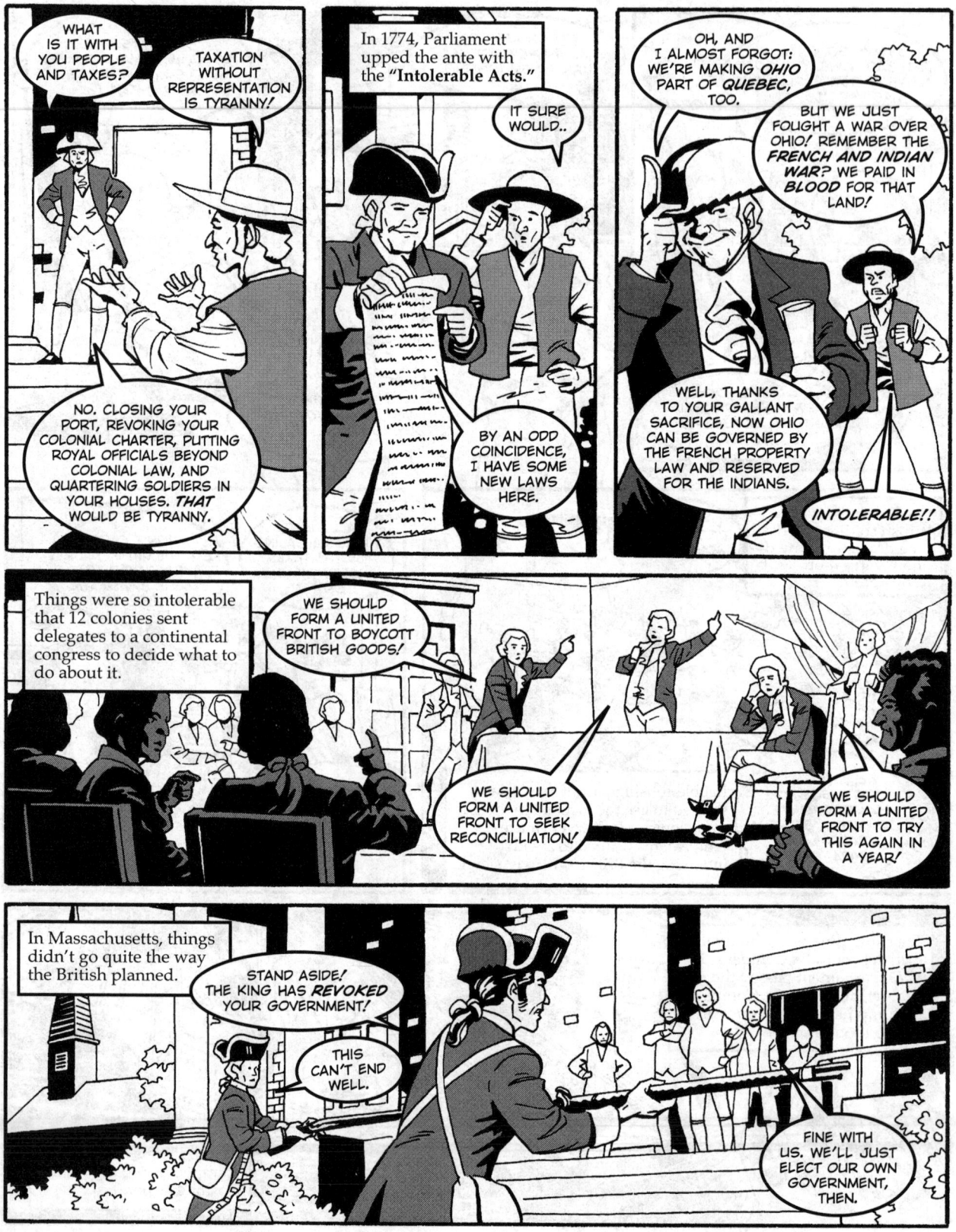
WHAT IS IT WITH YOU PEOPLE AND TAXES?
TAXATION WITHOUT REPRESENTATION IS TYRANNY!
NO. CLOSING YOUR PORT, REVOKING YOUR COLONIAL CHARTER, PUTTING ROYAL OFFICIALS BEYOND COLONIAL LAW, AND QUARTERING SOLDIERS IN YOUR HOUSES. THAT WOULD BE TYRANNY.
In 1774, Parliament upped the ante with the "Intolerable Acts."
IT SURE WOULD..
BY AN ODD COINCIDENCE, I HAVE SOME NEW LAWS HERE.
OH, AND I ALMOST FORGOT: WE'RE MAKING OHIO PART OF QUEBEC, TOO.
BUT WE JUST FOUGHT A WAR OVER OHIO! REMEMBER THE FRENCH AND INDIAN WAR? WE PAID IN BLOOD FOR THAT LAND!
WELL, THANKS TO YOUR GALLANT SACRIFICE, NOW OHIO CAN BE GOVERNED BY THE FRENCH PROPERTY LAW AND RESERVED FOR THE INDIANS.
INTOLERABLE!!
Things were so intolerable that 12 colonies sent delegates to a continental congress to decide what to do about it.
WE SHOULD FORM A UNITED FRONT TO BOYCOTT BRITISH GOODS!
WE SHOULD FORM A UNITED FRONT TO SEEK RECONCILLIATION!
WE SHOULD FORM A UNITED FRONT TO TRY THIS AGAIN IN A YEAR!
In Massachusetts, things didn't go quite the way the British planned.
STAND ASIDE! THE KING HAS REVOKED YOUR GOVERNMENT!
THIS CAN'T END WELL.
FINE WITH US. WE'LL JUST ELECT OUR OWN GOVERNMENT, THEN.

... AND I ADVISE YOU TO STOCKPILE GUNPOWDER-- AVAILABLE FROM ANY HANCOCK OUTLET-- JUST IN CASE.
Sam Adams and **John Hancock** made sure that all their fellow patriots knew about it, too.
"STOCKPILE GUNPOWDER"? SOUNDS LIKE REBELLION TO ME.
NICE SIGNATURE, THOUGH.
The British had to do something about Adams' and Hancock's growing network of arms depots and patriot "**minutemen.**"
GET READY TO SEIZE THE REBEL STOCKPILE. BUT DON'T ROUSE THEIR SUSPICIONS.
NO PROBLEM. I'LL JUST GATHER 700 MEN, MARCH THEM TO THE THIRD BUSIEST HARBOR IN THE COUNTRY, THROUGH AN ENTIRE CITY THAT HATES US, THEN SAIL UP THE RIVER IN PITCH BLACKNESS, ASKING DIRECTIONS IF WE SHOULD GET LOST.
WHAT COULD GO WRONG?
But somehow, the patriots uncovered the British plan.
And riders like **Paul Revere** got the word to the minutemen.
THE BRITISH ARE COMING!!
AREN'T WE STILL BRITISH?
YOU KNOW WHAT I MEAN!

STAND YOUR GROUND! IF THEY MEAN TO HAVE A WAR, LET IT BEGIN HERE!
And the minutemen were ready at Lexington ... with six hours warning.

I DON'T THINK WE QUITE DESTROYED ALL THE REBELS' WEAPONS.
And they were even readier at Concord.

And the militia kept assembling ...
... and assembling ...
... until 15,000 patriots had showed up to besiege the redcoats in Boston.

The British got reinforcements, too, along with a new general, William Howe.

WHICH ONE IS BUNKER HILL, AGAIN?
THE STRATEGIC ONE, STUPID.
WHICH ONE IS THE STRATEGIC ONE, AGAIN?
The patriots decided to move in and seize strategic Bunker Hill just outside the city.

Howe had to attack. The British took the hill at the cost of over a thousand casualties. It turned out to be Breed's Hill after all.
DON'T FIRE 'TIL YOU SEE THE WHITES OF THEIR EYES!

Meanwhile, in Philadelphia, the Second Continental Congress found itself with a war to run.
WE SHOULD SEND A PETITION TO THE KING!
WE SHOULD ...
WHAT DID YOU SAY?
IT HAS TO BE A VIRGINIA PLANTER-- SOUTHERN SUPPORT FOR A NEW ENGLAND REBELLION WILL BE CRUCIAL.
I COULD MOVE TO VIRGINIA.
OR ...
And John Adams found them someone to run it:
George Washington of Virginia. Washington was a respected congressman and Virginia politician – with military experience in the French and Indian War.
In fact, he was the one who *started* the French and Indian War.
Somehow, Washington turned the besieging militia into a Continental Army. Mostly by running off anyone who didn't want to be in an army.
TEN-HUT!
WHO PUT *HIM* IN CHARGE?
WELL, *I* DIDN'T VOTE FOR HIM.
In March of 1776, Washington took Boston from the British without firing a shot.
And in September, he lost New York City to the British the same way.

SO THE KING DIDN'T EVEN LOOK AT OUR PETITION.
SO ... WHAT NOW?
But what was the war about?

IS LIFE SO DEAR, OR PEACE SO SWEET, AS TO BE PURCHASED AT THE PRICE OF CHAINS AND SLAVERY? FORBID IT, ALMIGHTY GOD! I KNOW NOT WHAT COURSE OTHERS MAY TAKE; BUT AS FOR ME, GIVE ME LIBERTY OR GIVE ME DEATH!
What did Patrick Henry mean when he said this, on March 23, 1775?

THE KING, OR MORE LIKELY HIS EVIL MINISTERS, HAVE VIOLATED OUR LIBERTIES, THOSE POSSESSED BY ALL LOYAL ENGLISHMEN!
Did he mean what virtually all Americans, and even most patriots, meant? Or something more radical?

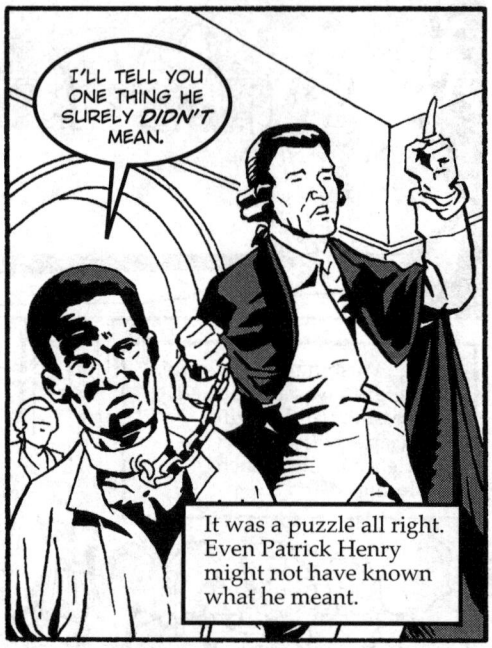
I'LL TELL YOU ONE THING HE SURELY DIDN'T MEAN.
It was a puzzle all right. Even Patrick Henry might not have known what he meant.

"THERE IS SOMETHING EXCEEDINGLY RIDICULOUS IN THE COMPOSITION OF MONARCHY ... EVERY THING THAT IS RIGHT OR NATURAL PLEADS FOR SEPARATION. THE BLOOD OF THE SLAIN, THE WEEPING VOICE OF NATURE CRIES, 'TIS TIME TO PART!... IN AMERICA, THE LAW IS KING!"
But Thomas Paine – a radical friend of Ben Franklin's, just arrived from England – knew.

"... THERE IS SOMETHING VERY ABSURD IN SUPPOSING A CONTINENT TO BE PERPETUALLY GOVERNED BY AN ISLAND."
WHY, THAT'S JUST COMMON SENSE!
OH, SO YOU'VE READ IT ALREADY.
Paine's pamphlet Common Sense sold half a million copies. One in every four Americans bought a copy.

RESOLVED, THAT THESE UNITED COLONIES ARE, AND OF RIGHT OUGHT TO BE, FREE AND INDEPENDENT STATES, THAT THEY ARE ABSOLVED FROM ALL ALLEGIANCE TO THE BRITISH CROWN, AND THAT ALL POLITICAL CONNECTION BETWEEN THEM AND THE STATE OF GREAT BRITAIN IS, AND OUGHT TO BE, TOTALLY DISSOLVED.
And as it changed public opinion, Congress followed.

When in the Course of human events, it becomes necessary for one people to dissolve the political bands which have connected them with another, and to assume among the powers of the earth, the separate and equal station to which the Laws of Nature and of Nature's God entitle them, a decent respect to the opinions of mankind requires that they should declare the causes which impel them to the separation. We hold these truths to be self evident, that all men are created equal, that they are endowed by their Creator with certain inalienable Rights, that among these are Life, Liberty and the pursuit of Happiness. That to secure these rights, Governments are instituted among Men, deriving their just powers from the consent of the governed, That whenever any Form of Government becomes destructive of these ends, it is the Right of the People to alter or to abolish it, and to institute new Government...

But at the end, it was still Jefferson's. And America's. And the world's.

And 55 others signed it, over the next year. Nine signers, and the son of another, would die during the war. The British imprisoned 5 signers, and 12 lost their homes. All of them risked a hangman's noose.

And for the support of this Declaration, with a firm reliance on the protection of divine Providence, we mutually pledge to each other our Lives, our Fortunes and our sacred Honor.

Meanwhile, the Continental Army was seeing how much continent it could put between itself and the British.
By the time they reached Pennsylvania, the entire Continental Army was down to 2,400 men.
So, of course, Washington attacked.
On Christmas Night, 1776, Washington crossed the Delaware with just 500 men under his command.
He surprised the garrison of Hessians – German mercenaries working for the British – at Trenton.
And he really surprised Lord Cornwallis a week later at Princeton.
But nobody in 1777 was more surprised than the British General Burgoyne. He marched south out of Canada to rendezvous with General Howe's forces marching north from New York.
WHERE IS EVERYONE?
Instead, he rendezvoused with 15,000 American soldiers at Saratoga.
America's victory at Saratoga convinced the French to get into the war.
HOW BETTER TO WEAKEN OUR BRITISH ENEMIES THAN TO COME TO AMERICA'S AID?
YOUR MAJESTY HAS AN EXCELLENT HEAD ON HIS SHOULDERS.
BUT FOR HOW LONG?

The Indians, meanwhile, were (mostly) coming into the war on the British side.
CALL IT A PREMONITION ...
... BUT SOMEHOW I DON'T THINK THE REBELS REALLY HAVE OUR BEST INTERESTS AT HEART.
So the Americans brought the war to them. Washington ordered General Sullivan to crush the Iroquois at all costs.
DID YOU KNOW THAT WASHINGTON'S SENECA NAME IS "TOWN BURNER"?
SOMEHOW I GUESSED IT MIGHT BE
The Shawnee and Daniel Boone fought over Kentucky.
I'M BEGINNING TO THINK WE SHOULDN'T HAVE ADOPTED YOU INTO THE TRIBE AFTER ALL.
And in the South, Dragging Canoe led the Cherokee against the colonists.
I KIND OF GET WHY THE WHITES LIKE DOING THIS SO MUCH.
By 1779, the rest of the British war effort was in the South, because Washington had them stalemated in the North.

BRANDYWINE
GERMANTOWN
MONMOUTH
The British had won (or nearly won) every battle … but every time, Washington kept his army alive to fight the next one … and the British pulled a little bit further back to New York.
GUILFORD COURTHOSE
NINETY-SIX
EUTAW SPRINGS
In the South, American General Nathanael Greene lost (or nearly lost) every battle … but after each "win," the British were a little bit weaker … and a little bit further from their supplies.
Lord Cornwallis, the British commander, decided to march to the nearest port.
LITTLE FOOD, LESS AMMUNITION, AND WINTER COMING ON?
WHAT DO THEY THINK WE ARE, CONTINENTALS?
Yorktown, in Virginia.
THIS TOWN IS IMPREGNABLE. WHY, IT WOULD REQUIRE A FRENCH NAVAL SQUADRON AND A MILITARY GENIUS TO TAKE IT FROM ME!
Then the French fleet cut the British supply line.
And Washington and the French army linked up.
LAFAYETTE, THEY ARE HERE!
And Cornwallis was really surprised one last time. He surrendered to George Washington on October 19, 1781. The band played "The World Turned Upside Down."

The Continental Army had Yorktown, and it had the French army, but there was one thing it didn't have – money.
The Continental Congress had no power to tax, depending on voluntary contributions from the states.
WE CAN BARELY PAY OURSELVES!
The money the Congress printed, therefore, was "not worth a Continental" – by 1781, it took 186 paper dollars to equal one gold dollar.
And even when Congress did pay the troops, it was with worthless paper dollars.
THERE YOU GO, BRAVE FELLOW!
This did not endear Congress to the army.
In March of 1783, Continental officers at Newburgh, New York, proposed that Washington should either lead the army into Ohio to start their own country, or march on Congress to demand back pay, or make himself King of America and do … anything he wanted.
THIS DREADFUL ALTERNATIVE, OF EITHER DESERTING OUR COUNTRY IN THE EXTREMEST HOUR OF HER DISTRESS OR TURNING OUR ARMS AGAINST IT … HAS SOMETHING SO SHOCKING IN IT THAT HUMANITY REVOLTS AT THE IDEA.
Washington rejected the scheme, shamed its authors, and incidentally saved America yet again.

Meanwhile, in England, the surrender at Yorktown had isolated George III and the war party. A new government just wanted to get the war over with.
So they signed the Treaty of Paris in 1783, giving America everything it asked for.
I WANTED CANADA, TOO, BUT I SETTLED FOR EVERYTHING ELSE.
Both sides ignored the Treaty where they could. The British kept six forts on the Great Lakes.
And they didn't return the escaped slaves who had fled to British lines during the war. British General Carleton freed 3,000 of them in Canada.
SO SORRY, OLD CHAP, BUT THEY'VE GOT THESE DASHED INALIENABLE RIGHTS, DON'T YOU KNOW?
Congress, meanwhile, ignored the part of the Treaty that called for "restitution" for property looted from the Tories, or Loyalists.
PAY OFF THE TORIES? WE CAN'T EVEN PAY OUR SOLDIERS!
WE CAN PAY 'EM IN TAR. OR FEATHERS.
About 15% of Americans had stayed loyal to King George during the war, and some had even raised their own militias to fight the patriots.
This turned out to be an unwise decision.
ENGLAND
About 70,000 Loyalists left home – and America – entirely.

Not that America was such a great place to be, just after the war. Trade with Britain was in a shambles. All the debt Congress ran up during the war, and all those paper Continentals, crashed the economy.
WE'RE READY TO BUY TEA NOW...
TEA
In 1785, Pennsylvania revoked the charter of Congress' bank. Congress – which still had no taxing power – could no longer pay the army or the navy.
WILL PASS UNENFORCABL LAWS FOR FOOD
The states, meanwhile, made sure they collected their taxes – in hard money. Farmers who had borrowed paper money were in a hard place.
PAY YOUR TAXES IN HARD MONEY, OR LOSE YOUR LAND.
BUT I DON'T HAVE ANY GOLD.
THAT'S WHY THEY CALL IT "HARD MONEY."
Thousands of farmers just went west, to start over again. Hundreds went to debtor's prison.
THE GOVERNMENT TOOK MY LAND AWAY AT GUNPOINT!
YOU DON'T SAY.
But some of them – including some unpaid veterans of the Revolution – had other ideas. In Massachusetts, Captain Daniel Shays led 9,000 farmers in a tax revolt ...
LESS TAXATION, MORE REPRESENTATION!
... and into the guns of a private militia hired by Governor Bowdoin of Massachusetts.
Former tax protestor Sam Adams called for Shays and his men to be hung for treason.
REBELLION AGAINST A KING MAY BE PARDONED, OR LIGHTLY PUNISHED, BUT THE MAN WHO DARES TO REBEL AGAINST THE LAWS OF A REPUBLIC OUGHT TO SUFFER DEATH!'"
After the fracas died down, Massachusetts elected a different governor – John Hancock – who pardoned Shays' rebels instead.
WHAT TOOK GOVERNOR HANCOCK SO LONG?
YOU KNOW HOW MUCH TIME IT TAKES HIM TO SIGN SOMETHING.

Congress still worked – when it did – under the Articles of Confederation.
ALL THOSE IN FAVOR OF LOOKING UNDER OUR CHAIRS FOR MORE MONEY...
AYE.
NAY.
AYE.
NAY.
AYE.
AYE.
AYE.
AYE.
NAY.
AYE.
NAY.
NAY.

It had no judiciary. It had no currency, with its bank out of business. And it required 9 votes to pass anything.
BY A VOTE OF 8 AYES TO 5 NAYS, THE MOTION FAILS.

Congress couldn't regulate trade, either. And with no national courts, trade disputes between states could never be settled. Some states began to boycott each other.
SPOONS
FORK
FOR
SAL

Your sentiments that our affairs are drawing rapidly to a crisis, accord with my own. What the event will be, is also beyond the reach of my foresight.
Boycotts, tax revolts ... it was starting to look way too familiar.

A little rebellion now and then is a good thing. It is a medicine necessary for the sound health of government. God forbid that we should ever be twenty years without such a rebellion.
Thomas Jefferson didn't mind so much ... but of course he was safe in France.

Jefferson's protégé James Madison disagreed. He called for a convention in Annapolis to settle the states' ongoing trade disputes.
There Madison joined forces with Alexander Hamilton, the illegitimate son of a West Indian clerk. Hamilton was Washington's trusted aide during the war, and fought well at Trenton and Yorktown.

The Annapolis Convention agreed on one thing at least – there should be another convention.

So, Madison and Hamilton between them got 12 states to send delegates to another convention in Philadelphia, to amend the Articles of Confederation, and to get it right this time. They made two good moves right up front.
They elected George Washington to preside over the Convention.
ALL THOSE IN FAVOR?
AYE
AYE
AYE
AYE
AYE
AYE
AYEP
AYE
AYUH
AYE
AYE
AYE
AYE
And they voted not to tell anyone else what they were doing.
NO PRESS. LOTS OF RUM.
BICAMERAL!
LIFELONG TERMS!
MULTIPLE EXECUTIVES!
ABSOLUTE VETO!
NO STANDING ARMY!
NO VETO OF STATE LAWS!
So it might have gone something like this… After all, there were 35 lawyers in the room.

Or maybe it went more like this… It was very hot in there, after all.
OKAY, HOW ABOUT TWO HOUSES? THE HOUSE CAN BE REPRESENTATIVE, BASED ON POPULATION, AND EACH STATE GETS ONE VOTE IN THE SENATE.
MAKE IT TWO VOTES.
SOUNDS GOOD.
WORKS FOR ME.
HEY, FRANKLIN, WHY DON'T YOU INVENT SOMETHING USEFUL LIKE AIR CONDITIONING?
FINE. ANYTHING.
WHERE'S THAT BOY WITH THE RUM?
Not all the compromises would be that easy.
WHAT ARE YOU ALL ARGUING ABOUT NOW?
ER, UM … JUST LEAVE IT THERE AND WE'LL SETTLE UP LATER, WILL YOU?
SLAVERY IS SLOW POISON! IT CONTAMINATES OUR MIND AND MORALS!
HOW MANY SLAVES DO YOU OWN, ANYWAY, GEORGE?
THAT'S NOT THE POINT.
So slaves still counted as "three fifths of a person" for representation. And the Constitution never used the word "slavery" at all.
I MOVE WE LEAVE EVERYTHING LIKE IT IS NOW EXCEPT WE ABOLISH THE SLAVE TRADE IN 20 YEARS.
SECONDED.
SECOND.
SECOND.
SECOND.
Since everybody knew who was going to be the first president anyway, the Convention went along with Hamilton's strong executive.
FINE, WE'LL ONLY HAVE ONE PRESIDENT AT A TIME.
ELECTED BY POPULAR VOTE … ER, BY ELECTORS ELECTED POPULARLY … ER …
I STILL SAY WE SHOULD JUST ELECT HIM FOR LIFE.

After four hot, stuffy months, the Constitution was done.
"WE THE PEOPLE ..."
BRANCHES OF GOVERNMENT
LEGISLATIVE
EXECUTIVE
JUDICIAL
IT ASTONISHES ME, SIR, TO FIND THIS SYSTEM APPROACHING SO NEAR TO PERFECTION AS IT DOES; AND I THINK IT WILL ASTONISH OUR ENEMIES.
I FEEL LIKE WE FORGOT SOMETHING...
WHERE'S OUR INALIENABLE RIGHTS, YOU MONARCHIST LAP DOGS?!?
Ratification would not be easy.

There were a lot of arguments against the Constitution.
CONGRESS WILL STRANGLE COMMERCE!
IT'S A POWER-GRAB BY CONGRESS!
BILL OF RIGHTS!
THE PRESIDENT IS BUT A KING RE-NAMED!
NO TAXES!
NO ARMIES!
BILL OF RIGHTS!
ONLY THE RICH WANT IT!
BILL OF RIGHTS!
I AM PUBLIUS.
I AM KOFF PUBLIUS.
I AM PUBLIUS.
But the pro-ratification side was unified.
And it had one big thing in its favor.
Five states ratified the Constitution in the first two months.
I DON'T CARE. I'M NOT SIGNING ANY CONSTITUTION UNLESS IT HAS A BILL OF RIGHTS IN IT.
AND HE'S VERY GOOD AT SIGNING THINGS, YOU KNOW.
Starting with Massachusetts, 4 more states ratified the Constitution – but only on the condition that a Bill of Rights be added to it.
SO WRITE A BILL OF RIGHTS. JUST COPY VIRGINIA'S.
BUT I DON'T WANT ONE! I HAVE WRITER'S CRAMP! MAKE GEORGE MASON DO IT!
IF YOU DON'T, WE HAVE TO GO LOCK OURSELVES INDOORS IN PHILADELPHIA ALL NEXT SUMMER, TOO.
I. Freedom of religion, speech, the press, and assembly
II. Right to keep and bear arms
III. No quartering troops in civilian homes
IV. No unreasonable search and seizure
V. Due process: no double jeopardy, self-incrimination, forfeiture of property
VI. Speedy trial by jury and rights of the accused to defense
VII. Civil trial by jury
VIII. No excessive bail or cruel and unusual punishment
IX. This list is not complete
X. All powers not expicitly granted the Federal government are reserved for the people
And so they were. And everybody's rights lived happily ever after.

The Electoral College unanimously voted for George Washington in 1789, making him the first President of the United States.
WASHINGTON ...
WASHINGTON ...
WASHINGTON ...
ADAMS ... JUST KIDDING ...
WASHINGTON ...
Washington appointed Jefferson Secretary of State, and Hamilton Secretary of the Treasury.
Hamilton immediately set to work fixing the debt crisis.
THE FEDERAL GOVERNMENT WILL BUY UP ALL THE STATE DEBT, AND BACK THE WHOLE NATIONAL DEBT WITH TARIFFS AND SALES OF WESTERN LAND.
THUS ENRICHING YOUR BANKER FRIENDS.
IT'S A WIN-WIN!
Jefferson hated the idea ... until Hamilton agreed to move the national capital from New York to the South.
THEN IT'S SETTLED. A NEW CAPITAL ON THE POTOMAC RIVER, NAMED ...
JEFFER-HAM, D.C.
HAMIL-JEFF, D.C.
Hamilton's new tariffs encouraged the growth of American industry. So did the opportunities available in America for English mill-workers ...
I THINK WE CAN FIX THIS WITH TWO SIMPLE STEPS, GUVNOR.
WHAT ARE THEY?
WELL, THE FIRST STEP IS TO PUT ME IN CHARGE.
YOU'LL ALL BE GLAD TO KNOW THAT WHITNEY'S COTTON GIN TAKES ALL THE WORK OUT OF CLEANING THE COTTON!
... and for American inventors and entrepreneurs like Eli Whitney.

One of Hamilton's new taxes was a very unpopular tax on whiskey.
NO, YOU CAN'T PAY THE TAX ON WHISKEY IN WHISKEY.
HOW 'BOUT I PAY IT IN LEAD, THEN?
In 1794, Washington called up 12,000 militia, and marched into Pennsylvania to put down the Whiskey Rebellion.
MR. PRESIDENT, THE REBELS HAVE PRETTY MUCH MELTED AWAY.
EXCELLENT. DECLARE VICTORY AND LET'S GO HOME.
BUT MR. PRESIDENT ...
TRUST ME, I KNOW HOW NOT TO FIGHT A BUNCH OF REBELS.
The army, meanwhile, was busy fighting a war with the Indians, who the British were supplying from the forts they still occupied on the Great Lakes.
War had also broken out in Europe – and in Washington's cabinet – between Britain and Revolutionary France.
WE MUST AID THE REVOLUTION IN FRANCE, AS FRANCE AIDED OUR REVOLUTION!
YOUR REVOLUTIONARIES HAVE BEHEADED THE KING WHO AIDED US! WE DEPEND ON TRADE WITH BRITAIN!
GREEDY MONARCHIST!
FOOLISH BUTCHER!
John Jay's treaty with Britain (to get those Great Lakes forts back) got tangled up in the brouhaha.
AYE TO JAY
NAY TO JAY
I FIND FOREIGN POLICY DISCUSSIONS SIMPLY FASCINATING, DON'T YOU?
The common and continual mischiefs of the spirit of party are sufficient to make it the interest and duty of a wise people to discourage and restrain it. It serves always to distract the Public Councils, and enfeeble the Public Administration. It agitates the Community with ill-founded jealousies and false alarms; kindles the animosity of one part against another.
Sick of the whole mess, Washington did his country another service – he refused to run for a third term as president and stepped down.

In 1796, John Adams, a Federalist (and Washington's grumpy vice president) was elected president by a narrow margin. The second-place candidate, Jefferson, became vice president, as the Constitution then required.
MISERABLE INGRATES. SEE IF I DEFEND *THEIR* LIBERTY AGAIN.
APPARENTLY NOT ENDOWED WITH INALIENABLE BRAINS.

After Congress approved Jay's Treaty, Britain stopped seizing American ships. So France *started* seizing American ships.

Adams sent an ambassador to France to negotiate … and when that didn't work, he began building up the navy.
MILLIONS FOR DEFENSE, BUT NOT ONE CENT FOR TRIBUTE!

So France and America fought an undeclared "quasi-war" at sea for two years.
I'M *QUASI-SHOT!*
I *UNDECLARE!*

Worried about French agents in America, in 1798 the Federalist Congress passed the Alien and Sedition Acts, allowing the president to deport dangerous aliens and outlawing "false, scandalous, and malicious writing" about the government.
BY A VOTE OF *44* TO *41*, THE ***SEDITION ACT*** PASSES.
IT'S A STUPID LAW, ANYWAY.
YOU'RE UNDER ARREST.

Adams deported nobody, and the amount of malicious writing about the government skyrocketed.
TYRANT!
OPPRESSOR!
MONARCHIST!

In 1800, Adams ran for re-election against his vice president, Jefferson.
Jefferson's running mate Aaron Burr, a Revolutionary War hero and by now Hamilton's rival in New York politics, swung New York's legislature to the Republicans that April.
IT'S PLAIN THAT BURR HAS USED HIS BANKING CONNECTIONS TO BUY THE ELECTION IN NEW YORK!
WHAT ARE YOU, JEALOUS THAT YOU DIDN'T THINK OF IT FIRST?
New York's votes put the Republicans over the top. But the Republican electors accidentally cast as many votes for Burr as they did Jefferson.
So the tied presidential election went into the House of Representatives … where Hamilton and the Federalists still had a lame-duck majority.
JEFFERSON IS BY FAR NOT SO DANGEROUS A MAN AS BURR.
TO WHOM?
TO HAMILTON.
Thus, Thomas Jefferson became the third president.
In 1804, the Twelfth Amendment split the presidential and vice-presidential ballots, so that this problem, at least, could not recur.
XII

On Adams' way out of office, however, he reformed the federal judiciary …
… by stocking it with Federalist judges, including the new Chief Justice, John Marshall.
MR. VICE PRESIDENT, WE FIND JUSTICE CHASE NOT GUILTY.
Jefferson and the Republicans fought back, impeaching the Federalist Supreme Court Justice Samuel Chase. Under Aaron Burr, now vice president, the Senate found Chase innocent.
With impeachment off the table, Republicans simply refused to issue commissions to Adams' appointees. One appointee, William Marbury, sued the government – specifically, Secretary of State James Madison – to get his commission certified.
THIS COURT FINDS PORTIONS OF THE *JUDICIARY ACT* OF 1789 UNCONSTITUTIONAL.
YOUR HONOR, I DON'T RECALL "JUDICIAL REVIEW" APPEARING IN THE CONSTITUTION.
OH, IT'S IN THERE. JUST LOOK FOR IT.
SERIOUSLY, YOUR HONOR, *I* WROTE THE THING. IT'S NOT IN THERE.
In *Marbury v. Madison,* the Supreme Court ruled that Marbury should have gotten his commission, but that the Court – despite what Congress had legislated – had no power to grant it. Marshall had established the Court's power to declare laws unconstitutional.

After the drama of the 1800 election, Jefferson decided to unify the nation and abandon some of his radical rhetoric.
WE ARE ALL REPUBLICANS. WE ARE ALL FEDERALISTS.
Jefferson did cut back the army and the navy, and let the Alien and Sedition Acts expire.
SOME OF MY BEST FRIENDS ARE SEDITIOUS ALIENS.
SO MUCH FOR THE TAX ON WHISKEY.
And he appointed the Swiss-born Albert Gallatin, a former spokesman for the Whiskey Rebellion, as Secretary of the Treasury. Gallatin cut all federal taxes to zero, funding the government – what there was left of it – from tariffs alone.
Jefferson did his best to make the presidency more democratic. He cut out fancy balls and state dinners, answered all his mail personally, and welcomed all visitors in informal style.
JUST SIT ANYWHERE.
I AM A WRITER, YOU KNOW.
Some days, perhaps, a little too informal.

In March of 1803, Ohio became the 17th state of the Union, pushing the northwestern frontier back to the Wabash River. Like the other western states and territories, all its goods had to be shipped downriver through New Orleans.
NO FRENCH, NO INDIANS! HOORAW!
While New Orleans was owned by Spain, that was bad enough.
EL RIO ESTA CERRADA HOY.
But in 1800, Napoleon took New Orleans back for France, intending to make it the capital of a new French empire in America – just as soon as his invincible armies put down a pesky rebellion in the rich sugar colony of Haiti.
YOUR MAJESTY, I'M THINKING OF ADDING LOUISIANA TO THE FRENCH EMPIRE.
WHAT? YOU CAN'T DO THAT! LOUISIANA IS SPANISH!
NOW I'M THINKING OF ADDING SPAIN TO THE FRENCH EMPIRE.
OH, WELL, IF YOU PUT IT THAT WAY ...
Jefferson sent James Monroe to France to buy New Orleans for $10 million. Napoleon had no interest in selling ...
... until Haiti had chewed through two or three invincible French armies.
With the British on the warpath again, Napoleon needed money and armies for his original French empire, the one in Europe. So he offered Monroe all of Louisiana for $15 million, cash on the barrelhead.
I COULD HAVE SWORN I HAD $ 15 MILLION IN HERE LAST WEEK.
Jefferson was torn ...
U.S. CONSTITUTION
THE CONSTITUTION HAS MADE NO PROVISION FOR INCORPORATING FOREIGN TERRITORY ...
... BUT THINK OF ALL THAT LAND!!
... but not for long. On October 20, 1803, the Senate ratified the Louisiana Purchase, and the United States doubled in size overnight. The frontier stretched a lot further from Ohio now.

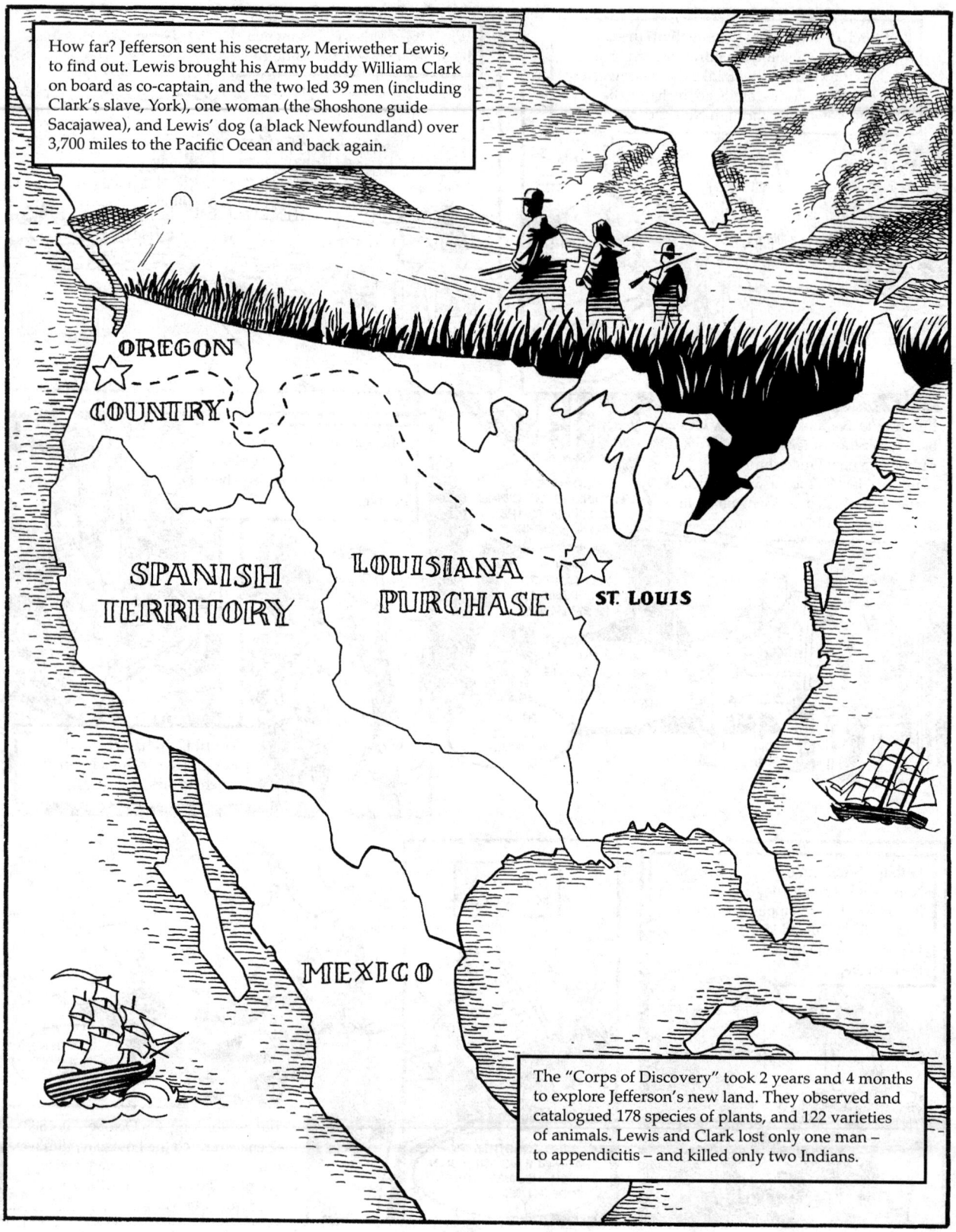
How far? Jefferson sent his secretary, Meriwether Lewis, to find out. Lewis brought his Army buddy William Clark on board as co-captain, and the two led 39 men (including Clark's slave, York), one woman (the Shoshone guide Sacajawea), and Lewis' dog (a black Newfoundland) over 3,700 miles to the Pacific Ocean and back again.
OREGON COUNTRY
SPANISH TERRITORY
LOUISIANA PURCHASE
ST. LOUIS
MEXICO
The "Corps of Discovery" took 2 years and 4 months to explore Jefferson's new land. They observed and catalogued 178 species of plants, and 122 varieties of animals. Lewis and Clark lost only one man – to appendicitis – and killed only two Indians.

The Louisiana Purchase further marginalized New England Federalists. Some of them talked about seceding from the Union.
WOULD WE HAVE MORE ROOM IN OUR OWN COUNTRY?
NO, BUT THE MAPS WOULD BE LARGER-SCALE.
According to Alexander Hamilton, some of them talked about it with Aaron Burr, who was running for Governor of New York. Hamilton's innuendo cost Burr the election.
BURR IS A REPROBATE.
BURR IS DISHONEST.
BURR IS A CONSPIRATOR.
BURR IS CORRUPT.
But it didn't stop there: Hamilton told some friends that he had a "still more despicable opinion" of Burr than that.
BUT WHAT'S WORSE ...
PSSS PSSS PSS
In 1804, those were fighting words. Vice President Burr challenged Hamilton to a duel and, on July 11, 1804, shot and killed him.
Suddenly everyone's opinion of Burr was despicable.
WANTED FOR MURDER
WANTED FOR TREASON
According to Thomas Jefferson, in 1806 Burr connived at conquering the Southwest and Louisiana for himself, and invading Mexico to boot.
ACCORDING TO THE CONSTITUTION, A CONVICTION FOR TREASON REQUIRES AN OVERT ACT.
NOT GUILTY.
OH, NOW HE READS IT LITERALLY.
Burr was charged with treason. In 1807, John Marshall tried the case, and Burr was found not guilty under the Constitution.

The new lands brought new settlers. Farmers from Virginia and North Carolina, where tobacco was getting less profitable, tried planting cotton and sugar cane in Mississippi and Louisiana.
I DON'T KNOW ... SOMETHING'S MISSING ...
As new, more fertile lands opened up for cotton cultivation in the Deep South, so did an internal slave trade. Slave traders force-marched 10,000 or more slaves per year across the South to new plantations.
WE'VE GOT TO GO TO ALABAMA, BOYS, THE SOIL'S EXHAUSTED BACK IN VIRGINNY.
THE SOIL'S EXHAUSTED? WHAT ABOUT US?
Some got away, fleeing north to Canada or south to Indian territory in Florida.
The Constitution allowed the overseas slave trade for 20 years after ratification. In 1807, Jefferson signed a bill banning the importation of slaves.
PROTECTING DOMESTIC INDUSTRY, MISTER PRESIDENT? HOW HAMILTONIAN OF YOU.
We have the wolf by the ears, and we can neither hold him, nor safely let him go. Justice is in one scale, and self-preservation in the other.
Jefferson was tormented by the issue. He helped make sure the Northwest Territory was free soil. His writings repeatedly condemned slavery, while deprecating black intelligence and urging their deportation. Unlike Washington, he could not even free his slaves even when he died.
Jefferson's writings may even have inspired one Virginia slave rebellion, that of Gabriel Prosser in 1800.
JEFFERSON SAYS IF HE WINS THE ELECTION, HE'LL FREE THE WORKERS FROM FEDERALIST SLAVERY.
YOU THINK THAT ONE'S GOOD, YOU OUGHTA READ THE ONE ABOUT HOW "ALL MEN ARE CREATED EQUAL."

If Jefferson couldn't, or wouldn't, free any slaves at home, there was one place where he could and would.
GEORGIA?
CLOSE...
The "Barbary States" of North Africa had been capturing European ships and enslaving the crews since the 1500s – and once there were American crews to enslave, they captured them, too.
AMERICANS? WHAT ARE THEY WORTH?
I DON'T KNOW, EFFENDI - THEY'RE NOT IN THE PRICE GUIDE.
Congress had to budget about $1 million a year to pay sailors' ransoms, or to bribe the Barbary States not to attack American ships in the first place.
AMERICANS TAKEN TO AFRICA AS SLAVES? WHY, THAT'S ... UNNATURAL!
With Jefferson cutting budgets, this line item – approximately 20% of U.S. government revenue in 1800 – was chopped. So the Pasha of Tripoli started attacking American ships again.
WELCOME BACK!
DON'T MENTION IT.
Jefferson had cut Adams' navy back, too, but he sent what there was left of it – four ships – to blockade and harass Barbary shipping.
WE NEED MORE SHIPS.
WELL, WE'VE GOT A MILLION DOLLARS WE DIDN'T HAVE LAST YEAR.
In 1804, Lieutenant Stephen Decatur bravely burned a captured American ship in Tripoli harbor, but eight ships (Jefferson had started growing the navy again) weren't enough to take Tripoli.
AND THERE'S SEVEN MORE WHERE THAT CAME FROM!
In 1805, though, 10 U.S. Marines (and about 500 local mercenaries) took the Tripolitan city of Derne from the land, and the Pasha panicked. He agreed to a treaty that ended the Barbary War. The Pasha got $60,000 in ransom, Jefferson got 300 American slaves freed, and the Marine Corps got a line for their hymn.
MEN, WE HAVE TWO OBJECTIVES. ONE: THE CITY OF DERNE. TWO: THE SHORES OF TRIPOLI.
THAT SECOND OBJECTIVE IS WAY CATCHIER.

Not all the naval news was that good. In 1807, the *HMS Leopard* attacked and captured the *USS Chesapeake* in order to draft, or "impress," four American sailors the British claimed were British citizens.
The British desperately needed sailors, as the naval war with France had been raging for 14 years on and off – mostly on. The Royal Navy impressed at least 6,000 Americans during the struggle. The British "Orders in Council" also forbade American trade with France – and the British seized American ships that violated them.
WE'LL JUST BE IMPRESSING ALL YOUR HANDS, THEN.
BUT WE NEED THOSE MEN TO WORK OUR SHIP!
AH, YES, YOUR SHIP. WHICH BRINGS ME TO MY SECOND POINT ...
So by 1807, the whole country was wild for war with Britain. Jefferson responded with an embargo instead – on everybody.
IF WE DON'T GO TO SEA, NOBODY CAN TAKE OUR SHIPS AND MEN, CAN THEY? STANDS TO REASON.
ER...
(Almost un-noticed in all the excitement this year, Robert Fulton's North River Steamboat became the first commercially viable steamship line in the world. All those sailing ships were about to become obsolete.)
The response was predictable. In fact, Gallatin predicted it.
I THINK WE'VE GIVEN THE LAW ENOUGH TIME TO WORK.
I AGREE. LET'S *IGNORE* IT.
So Jefferson responded by making it a crime to even think about breaking the embargo, and sent the military to enforce warrantless seizures of smuggling ships.
I'M SO GLAD I VOTED FOR JEFFERSON, AREN'T YOU?
ME, TOO- THOSE ALIEN AND SEDITION ACTS WERE TERRIBLE.
Congress repealed the Embargo Acts in 1809, on the last day of Jefferson's presidency. He gratefully turned things over to James Madison.

During all this turmoil, millions of Americans were "coming to Jesus" in the Revival Movement, also called the Second Great Awakening. The First Great Awakening began in Massachusetts in 1733; the Second began in Kentucky in 1800.
CAMP MEETING
THE LORD IS COMING!!
But it spread all across the West, carried by "circuit-riding" preachers to the new farms and towns.
Something like it was happening even farther west, too. A Shawnee Indian (and notorious drunkard) named Lalawethika suddenly put down the bottle and announced that he had received a vision from the Master of Life. He changed his name to Tenskwatawa, "the Open Door." The whites called him The Prophet.
Tenskwatawa got a lot of prestige by predicting a solar eclipse in 1806.
... EXCEPT FOR THE WHITE MAN'S ASTRONOMY BOOKS ...
THE MASTER OF LIFE WILL GIVE US OUR LAND BACK, AND MAKE US BULLETPROOF! ALL WE MUST DO IS THROW AWAY THE WHITE MAN'S THINGS!
He got even more prestige by denouncing his enemies – mostly Indians who wanted to deal with the whites – as witches.
And he got the most prestige of all by being the brother of Tecumseh, a brilliant warrior and politician.

Tecumseh slowly built an alliance of Indian tribes from Canada to Alabama to oppose the Americans, while Tenskwatawa rapidly built a mass religious movement centered on a new "Prophetstown" on the Tippecanoe River.
WE MUST UNITE OR DIE!
THE MASTER OF LIFE WILL MAKE YOU BULLETPROOF!
GOVERNOR, THERE ARE 2,000 INDIANS AT PROPHETSTOWN, AND MORE ARRIVE EVERY DAY.
INDIANS SETTLING THE WEST WHERE WHITE PEOPLE WANT TO LIVE? IT'S ... UNNATURAL!
The governor of the Indiana Territory, William Henry Harrison, was worried about the sheer number of Indians flooding into Prophetstown.
While Tecumseh was down South in 1811, Harrison marched up to Prophetstown to frighten the Indians off.
I CERTAINLY DON'T FEEL VERY FRIGHTENED.
Instead, the Indians attacked his fort on the Tippecanoe River at night. Harrison fought Tenskwatawa's men off – and burned Prophetstown to the ground for good measure.
I CERTAINLY DON'T FEEL VERY BULLETPROOF.
Tecumseh regrouped and helped the British take Detroit in 1812, but Harrison pursued him relentlessly.
I THINK THE MASTER OF LIFE WANTS US TO GO NORTH.
I CONCUR.
On October 5, 1813, American soldiers killed Tecumseh in Canada.

CANADA? WHAT ARE WE DOING IN CANADA?
It was a fair question. In fact, most of the militia refused to serve in Canada.
This made it hard to fight …
FOLLOW ME, MEN!
MEN?
Join up for
The War of 1812
See Exciting Canada!
No Military Experience Needed or Provided!
May Bring Own Gun!
The new president, James Madison, ended Jefferson's embargo, but the British still used their "Orders in Council" to justify hijacking American shipping and impressing sailors. Britain, meanwhile, needed all its strength to defeat Napoleon.
HIS MAJESTY'S GOVERNMENT HAS WITHDRAWN THE "ORDERS IN COUNCIL."
June 20, 1812
THIS COUNTRY IS NOW AT WAR WITH GREAT BRITAIN.
June 19, 1812
So both sides did the only logical thing.
August 1812
WAR!
It was that kind of war.
August 1812
ORDERS IN COUNCIL SUSPENDED
DON'T WORRY! WE CAN INVADE CANADA NOW!
And we saw how well that turned out.
BLIMEY, NOW WE'RE IMPRESSED!
The war at sea turned out better. It also produced one of the war's only memorable lines.

DON'T GIVE UP THE SHIP!
His men gave up the ship.
Despite this, Oliver Hazard Perry took up Lawrence's last words as a rallying cry.
DON'T GIVE UP THE SHIP!
DON'T GIVE UP THE SHIP!
And his ship sank underneath him. It was that kind of war.
But at least Perry won the Battle of Lake Erie.
WE HAVE MET THE ENEMY, AND THEY ARE OURS.
On the water, in general, America did pretty well.
WOT 'AVE YOU GOT, THEN? IRON SIDES?
HEY, THAT'S NOT A BAD IDEA! CHECK BACK IN FIFTY YEARS!
On the land … not so much
Oh, sure, the Americans burned York, Ontario (the future Toronto).
And then the British burned Washington, D.C.
OH SAY, DID YOU SEE THAT ONE?
STOP DISTRACTING ME. I'M WRITING A SONG.
But they couldn't burn Baltimore.

By now, the War of 1812 had dragged on into 1814. Both sides were tired of it, and the British had Napoleon to finish off.
WE'RE BURNED OUT!
So they signed the Treaty of Ghent, which ended the war, in December.
OH, I SAY, ARE WE STILL AT WAR WITH YOU COLONIALS? COME 'ROUND TUESDAY, AND WE'LL SORT THAT OUT.
But since it took six weeks for the news to cross the Atlantic, the British invasion fleet at New Orleans in January didn't know the war was over.
And neither did Andrew Jackson, a backwoods lawyer-general who had already fought the British (in 1780) and the Creek Indians (in 1813) and was eager to fight the British again.
THE BRITS KILLED MY MA! I AIM TO MAKE MA PROUD.
The overconfident British made plenty of mistakes on the attack.
WE BEAT NAPOLEON. HOW HARD CAN BEATING ANDREW JACKSON BE?
Andrew Jackson made none. The British took 2,000 casualties and didn't take New Orleans. America had a new national hero.
KILL 'EM!!
KILL 'EM FOR MA!

PART TWO

A HOUSE DIVIDED 1815-1865

"A house divided against itself cannot stand."
– Mark 3:25, as quoted by Abraham Lincoln, 1858

It didn't seem so divided when James Monroe was elected president in 1816. It was the "Era of Good Feelings."
AT NO PERIOD OF OUR POLITICAL EXISTENCE HAVE WE HAD SO MUCH CAUSE TO FELICITATE OURSELVES AT THE PROSPEROUS AND HAPPY CONDITION OF OUR COUNTRY.
Indeed, in 1820, Monroe won every electoral vote except one – and that was only so that Washington would remain the sole unanimously elected president.
America settled on a flag design, too. In 1818, the flag went back to 13 stripes, and added only stars for new states thereafter. (It added five stars during Monroe's Presidency.)
Andrew Jackson felt so good he invaded Florida; in 1819 Monroe bought it from the Spanish.
NOT MUCH OF A WAR ... I'VE ONLY KILLED TWO BRITISHERS.
The Spanish were losing most of their colonies, though not, in most cases, to Andrew Jackson.
I'M THE GEORGE WASHINGTON OF SOUTH AMERICA- EXCEPT FOR THE DECLARING MYSELF DICTATOR PART!
Secretary of State John Quincy Adams wrote the "Monroe Doctrine" to warn Europe not to try re-colonizing them, either.
THE AMERICAN CONTINENTS, BY THE FREE AND INDEPENDENT CONDITION WHICH THEY HAVE ASSUMED AND MAINTAIN, ARE HENCEFORTH NOT TO BE CONSIDERED AS SUBJECTS FOR FUTURE COLONIZATION BY ANY EUROPEAN POWERS....
WHAT ABOUT BY NORTH AMERICAN POWERS?
I'LL HAVE TO GET BACK TO YOU ON THAT.

What sectional rivalry there was, was expressed by the Congressional Great Triumvirate: Henry Clay of Kentucky, Daniel Webster of Massachusetts, and John C. Calhoun of South Carolina.

The core policy of the Monroe administration was "The American System," which had three basic elements.

FOUR, IF YOU COUNT NAMING IT "THE AMERICAN SYSTEM."

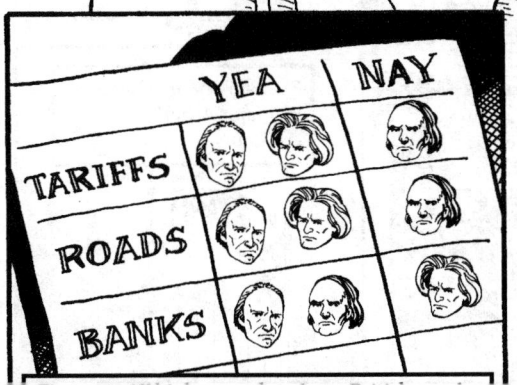

First, a tariff high enough to keep British goods out and support American industry. Second, national roads for internal trade. Third, a central bank to control the money supply.

In *McCulloch v. Maryland* in 1819, John Marshall ruled that the states could not regulate the Bank of the United States – the central government was supreme.

FEDERALISM ISN'T DEAD UNTIL I AM!

But states and private companies built their own "internal improvements," such as the Erie Canal …

… and the Baltimore & Ohio Railroad. (Although when it opened in January of 1830, the track was just a mile and a half long.)

Sectional problems worked out in compromise, as with the Missouri Compromise of 1820.

And when the uncompromising Andrew Jackson won the most votes in 1824 – but not enough for a majority in the four-way election -- Henry Clay's control of Congress gave the presidency to John Quincy Adams.

America was a young country – literally. The average age was 17. Of the U.S. 1830 population of 12.8 million, 11 million had been born since 1792. It was the most dramatic "Baby Boom" in American history, and when the kids came of age, they turned the 1820s (and 1830s) into the "first Sixties."
Two-thirds of Harvard's class of 1823 were expelled for rioting; students bombed Yale in 1826.
Young men wore comfortable trousers, not confining breeches and hose.
Opium for the "China Trade" was cheap and plentiful.
Charmed with this potent drug, the exulted mind
All sense of woe delivers to the wind
It clears the cloudy front of wrinkled care
And soothes the bosom of despair
Conspiracy theorists blamed The Man.
ANTI-MASONIC PARTY HEADQUARTERS
Sylvester Graham invented health food in 1822.
FLOUR
HONEY
By 1845, there were over 50 major American communes.
BROOK FARM
The growing Second Great Awakening brought hundreds of thousands of young people to outdoor festivals and religious concerts.
MORE SOULS ARE MADE THAN SAVED THERE.
THE ANGEL SAID THE BOOK OF MORMON IS BURIED HERE!
THE SEVENTH-DAY ADVENT WILL COME IN 1844!
And it brought revelations to, among others, Joseph Smith (in 1827) and William Miller (in 1830).

ON MY ARRIVAL IN THE UNITED STATES THE RELIGIOUS ASPECT OF THE COUNTRY WAS THE FIRST THING THAT STRUCK MY ATTENTION; AND THE LONGER I STAYED THERE, THE MORE I PERCEIVED THE GREAT POLITICAL CONSEQUENCES RESULTING FROM THIS NEW STATE OF THINGS.
In 1835, the French aristocrat Alexis de Tocqueville concluded that religion and democracy in America reinforced each other.
And sure enough, the Second Great Awakening saw democracy expand. In 1800, only two states had universal white male suffrage. By 1828, only three states had property requirements for the vote.
VOTE HERE
Which was good news for the people's hero, Andrew Jackson. He swept into office on a landslide – and Martin Van Buren's New York political machine – in 1828.
10,000 Jackson supporters swept into Washington, and smashed all the china in the White House during the inaugural celebration.
QUITE A DEMOCRATIC PARTY, EH?
I LIKE THE SOUND OF THAT.
Jackson's "Democratic Party" re-elected him in 1832 on a platform of lower tariffs, but he didn't lower them enough for John Calhoun. South Carolina declared the tariffs nullified and refused to collect or pay them.
LIBERTY AND UNION, NOW AND FOREVER, ONE AND INSEPARABLE!
BUT WHAT OF THE AMERICAN SYSTEM?
COUNT ME OUT.
Jackson threatened to nullify South Carolina, but signed Henry Clay's Compromise Tariff. South Carolina backed down. And the crisis was over … for a while.
I WILL *HANG* THE FIRST MAN I CAN LAY MY HAND ON ENGAGED IN SUCH TREASONABLE CONDUCT, UPON THE FIRST TREE I CAN REACH.

But a new crisis was growing, as young radicals entered, and supercharged, the abolition movement. In 1831, 26-year-old William Lloyd Garrison started *The Liberator,* a newspaper that called for immediate emancipation and full citizenship for all blacks.

I WILL BE AS HARSH AS TRUTH, AND AS UNCOMPROMISING AS JUSTICE. ON THIS SUBJECT, I DO NOT WISH TO THINK, OR TO SPEAK, OR WRITE, WITH MODERATION. NO! NO! TELL A MAN WHOSE HOUSE IS ON FIRE TO GIVE A MODERATE ALARM ... BUT URGE ME NOT TO USE MODERATION IN A CAUSE LIKE THE PRESENT.

I AM IN EARNEST -- I WILL NOT EQUIVOCATE -- I WILL NOT EXCUSE -- I WILL NOT RETREAT A SINGLE INCH-- ***AND I WILL BE HEARD.***

That same year, the preacher Nat Turner led a slave rebellion in Virginia that killed 51 whites.

The mob response killed over 100 blacks, not including the 18 rebels hung by the state. All across the South, slave laws tightened.

Frederick Douglass violated those laws, first by teaching himself to read, and then by escaping north in 1838. In 1841, Garrison talked him into giving speeches, and Douglass became the world's best-known and most effective abolition speaker.

Other slaves fled south, to the Seminole lands in Florida, and joined up with the brilliant Seminole war chief Osceola. The Seminoles kept slaves, but recruited escaped blacks as allies.

With no more than 100 warriors, Osceola held off up to 9,000 U.S. troops for two years. After his capture while under a flag of truce in 1837, the Seminole Wars continued for five more years.

Osceola was resisting Jackson's new policy of "Indian Removal."
WHAT WAS THE OLD POLICY, THEN?
The Indian Removal Act of 1830 authorized the federal government to exchange the land the Indian nations owned east of the Mississippi for new land west of the Mississippi – and to forcibly remove them if they resisted.
BUT WE'RE THE "FIVE CIVILIZED TRIBES!" LOOK HOW CIVILIZED WE ARE -- WE HAVE SLAVES, EVEN!
In *Worcester v. Georgia,* John Marshall tried to stall the plan by ruling that state laws had no force on Indian land. But when Jackson stared him down, Marshall blinked.
MARSHALL HAS MADE HIS RULING -- NOW LET HIM ENFORCE IT!"
So it was all legal. Of about 60,000 Indians (and 2,000 slaves) relocated to Oklahoma along the "Trail of Tears," approximately 10,000 died of disease or other hardships. As Tocqueville sarcastically put it: "It is impossible to destroy men with more respect for the laws of humanity."
The Last of the Mohicans
James Fenimore Cooper
Meanwhile, 400,000 Americans wept when they read about the death of Uncas. While Andrew Jackson was closing the eastern frontier, James Fenimore Cooper was inventing the Western.

And, perhaps, the West was inventing America. The historian Frederick Jackson Turner wrote: "... that dominant individualism, working for good and for evil, and withal that buoyancy and exuberance which comes with freedom – these are traits of the frontier, or traits called out elsewhere because of the existence of the frontier."
The frontier changed America, and Americans changed the frontier, mostly into farmland. Good farmland was cheap: as low as $1.25 an acre in the Jacksonian era.
I'LL TAKE A PLUG OF TOBACCO, A BOTTLE OF WHISKEY, A POUND OF BEANS, AND AN ACRE OF PRIME FARMLAND.
THAT'S $2.65.
KEEP THE CHANGE.
Cyrus McCormick's mechanical reaper (1834) helped harvest those ever-growing farms.
John Deere's "sod-busting" steel plow (1837) tore up tough prairie soil to plant still more.
And just in case something else went wrong out West, Captain Samuel Colt's revolver (1836) was there to help.
Some farmers kept going west, even into the Mexican territory of Texas.
I DON'T LIKE HAVING ALL THESE GRINGOS IN OUR COUNTRY.
DON'T WORRY -- THEY'LL KEEP THE FRONTIER SAFE FROM AMERICAN INVASION.
DO YOU EVEN LISTEN TO THE WORDS COMING OUT OF YOUR MOUTH?
In 1835, General Santa Anna declared himself dictator of Mexico, triggering the Texas Revolution. The ruckus attracted still more American adventurers, such as former congressman Davy Crockett.
YOU ALL CAN GO TO HELL. I'M GOING TO TEXAS.

Santa Anna's invasion of Texas was delayed by a 13-day siege of the Alamo mission, in San Antonio. On March 6, 1836, the Alamo fell, and Santa Anna killed every one of its 183 Anglo and Tejano defenders – including Davy Crockett, Juan Seguin, and Jim Bowie.
Three weeks later, his forces killed 342 surrendered prisoners at Goliad.
Two escapees from the Goliad Massacre were present when Sam Houston captured Santa Anna with his army at San Jacinto on April 21, 1836. Texas became an independent republic.
REMEMBER THE ALAMO!!
REMEMBER GOLIAD!!

Meanwhile, Andrew Jackson was making war on the Bank of the United States. He vetoed its charter in 1832 and won a landslide re-election on that issue over the Whig Party candidate Henry Clay.
I'D RATHER BE RIGHT THAN PRESIDENT.
I DON'T KNOW, HENRY -- THE OTHER WAY 'ROUND IS PRETTY GREAT, TOO.
He still had to fire two secretaries of the Treasury before his attorney general, Roger Taney, volunteered to illegally remove the bank's federal funds.
SO IGNORING THE CONSTITUTION IS OKAY WITH YOU, EH, ROGER? HOW'D YOU LIKE TO BE CHIEF JUSTICE OF THE SUPREME COURT AFTER MARSHALL DIES?
So Jackson's successor, Martin Van Buren, was left holding the bag when the destruction of the bank brought on the Crash of 1837.
$
Angry voters went Whig in 1840, electing William Henry Harrison – "Old Tippecanoe" -- President.
I WAS BORN IN A LOG CABIN -- AND I'VE BURNED A WHOLE LOG CITY!
HARD CIDER
Wearing no overcoat, Harrison gave a two-hour inaugural address in a snowstorm – and made Vice President John Tyler the president 30 days later.
AND IN CONCLUSION ...
The biggest news of the Tyler administration was Samuel Morse's telegraph, which he perfected in 1844. The age of instant messaging was born.
"WHAT HATH GOD WROUGHT?"
"AFK BRB LOL."

The telegraph line brought news of the 1844 Whig and Democratic conventions in Baltimore to Washington, and eventually helped carry the news that Democrat James K. Polk had beaten Henry Clay.
TELEGRAM
Senator Clay coion still right stop still not president stop
Just before Polk took office, President Tyler annexed Texas.
lower tariff
create independent treassury
annex Oregon
~~annex Texas~~
annex California
need a new barn
Congress went along with Polk's plans for the tariff and the Treasury, and the British went along with his plans for Oregon.
FIFTY-FOUR FORTY OR FIGHT.
54°40
49°
WOULD YOU TAKE 49?
CANADA
OREGON COUNTRY
DONE AND DONE.
The Mexicans were less cooperative.
$ 20 MILLION.
...
$ 30 MILLION.
...
Polk sent half the U.S. Army into the disputed Texas borderland, in the hope that the Mexicans would do something impulsive and give him an excuse to declare war.
This time, the Mexicans cooperated.

And Polk had his war with Mexico.
MEXICO HAS SHED AMERICAN BLOOD UPON THE AMERICAN SOIL.
A month after war was declared, Captain John C. Fremont took over California with 60 men – and U.S. Naval support.
WHAT'S WITH THE BEAR ON THE FLAG?
CALIFORNIA REPUBLIC
IT TESTED WELL WITH KIDS AND WOMEN 24 TO 35.
Whigs, like Illinois congressman Abraham Lincoln, opposed the war, seeing it as a corrupt excuse to expand slavery. But the Democrats controlled Congress, and kept the war going.
... THE BLOOD OF THIS WAR, LIKE THE BLOOD OF ABEL, IS CRYING TO HEAVEN AGAINST HIM.
General Zachary Taylor invaded Mexico from Texas, and beat Santa Anna (back in charge of Mexico again) at the Battle of Buena Vista. In 1848, he would be the next war hero elected president.
ALL OF A SUDDEN, I FEEL VERY PRESIDENTIAL!
General Winfield Scott landed American Marines at Veracruz and marched them straight into the Halls of Montezuma. Mexico City fell to the American invaders in 1847.
In the end, Polk had what he wanted, over 13,000 American soldiers were dead, and Mexico accepted $15 million for half of its territory.
MEXICAN CESSION 1848
MEXICO

Settlers flowed into the new territories, along scouted routes like the Oregon Trail.
WELL, THE BROCHURE DID SAY "PLENTY OF FRESH WATER" ...

Chased out of the East by angry mobs, the Mormons blazed their own trail to the Great Salt Lake in 1847.
THIS IS THE RIGHT PLACE. DRIVE ON!
ARE YOU SURE, BRIGHAM? IT LOOKS AN AWFUL LOT LIKE *UTAH*.

And Sutter's Mill, California, enjoyed its last quiet morning on January 24, 1848.
THAT'S PECULIAR. THAT ROCK ALMOST LOOKS LIKE *GOLD*.

The California Gold Rush was on. In 1848, 6,000 people arrived at the diggings. In 1849, almost 90,000 "Forty-Niners" showed up – 30,000 of them from other countries. By 1852, California's non-Indian population was 250,000.

While America got more foreigners, it also got more American. It got a national sport in baseball …

… a national music by Stephen Foster …
OLD KENTUCKY HOME!
OH SUSANNA!
FREEBIRD!
CAMPTOWN RACES!

… and a national philosopher in Ralph Waldo Emerson. (Or possibly in his frequent lecture mate, P.T. Barnum.)
MAN IS A STREAM WHOSE SOURCE IS HIDDEN.
NEVER GIVE A SUCKER AN EVEN BREAK.
I LIKE THE SECOND GUY.

And all of a sudden, it had a national literature. But the biggest book of all was none of these …
HISTORY O
MOBY-DICK
LEAVES OF GRASS
HIAWATHA
THE RAVEN AND OTHER POEMS
THE SCARLET LETTER
WALDEN
ROGET'S THESAURUS
THE LAWS O THOUGHT
DISPENSATIONS

Harriet Beecher Stowe's anti-slavery novel *Uncle Tom's Cabin* sold 300,000 copies in 1852, and became the 19th century's best-selling novel in the world – except in the South, where it was banned. It supercharged the abolitionist movement in America and England.

Even before Stowe, women were very active in the abolitionist movement. So active that the International Anti-Slavery Convention in London threw them out and made them sit in the balcony.

LUCRETIA MOTT.

HOW DO YOU DO? I'M ELIZABETH CADY STANTON.

So they started their own movement. In 1848, Stanton, Mott, and other abolitionist women met in Seneca Falls, New York, and produced the "Declaration of Sentiments," setting forth the proposition that men and women are created equal.

TROUSERS! EQUALITY! I MAY FAINT.

But the women were overshadowed by the new crisis, as newly rich, newly populous California demanded entry to the Union as a free state. With help from Democratic Senator Stephen Douglas, in 1850 Henry Clay passed one last Compromise.

CALIFORNIA A FREE STATE.

POPULAR SOVEREIGNTY ON SLAVERY IN UTAH AND NEW MEXICO.

NO SLAVE TRADE IN D.C.

TOUGH FUGITIVE SLAVE LAWS.

This satisfied nobody. 1850 was not 1820: compromise was out of fashion. The young radicals had become middle-aged even-more-radicals.

SO PERISH ALL COMPROMISES WITH TYRANNY.

The new Fugitive Slave Act of 1850 was intended to clamp down on the Underground Railroad, by which radicals, preachers, and former slaves smuggled escapees through the North to freedom in Canada.

MY NAME IS HARRIET TUBMAN, AND I'LL BE YOUR CONDUCTOR TONIGHT. THE GOOD LORD IS OUR ENGINEER.

To make things still worse, the resolute President Taylor died in office in 1850 just as the crisis hit. The next three Presidents – Millard Fillmore, Franklin Pierce, and James Buchanan – might as well have been dead in office, for all the control they exercised over the onrushing catastrophe.

WELL, I *DID* OPEN JAPAN.

In 1854, the Kansas-Nebraska Act extended "popular sovereignty" to the Kansas and Nebraska Territories. Whichever side won the election would decide whether the territories were slave or free. Radicals on both sides poured into "Bleeding Kansas" to fight it out.

The Act split the Democrats and the Whigs, and led to the creation of the anti-slavery Republican Party.

FREE MEN!

FREE SOIL!

FREMONT!

WOULD YOU ACCEPT TWO OUT OF THREE?

THE NEGRO HAS NO RIGHTS THAT THE WHITE MAN IS BOUND TO RESPECT.

In 1856, Chief Justice Roger Taney overturned the Missouri Compromise in *Dred Scott v. Sanford.*

In national speeches and a series of debates with Stephen Douglas, former congressman Lincoln raised the Republican profile across the country.

I ASK YOU, ARE YOU IN FAVOR OF CONFERRING UPON THE NEGRO THE RIGHTS AND PRIVILEGES OF CITIZENSHIP?

IN THE RIGHT TO EAT THE BREAD, WITHOUT THE LEAVE OF ANYBODY ELSE, WHICH HIS OWN HAND EARNS, HE IS MY EQUAL AND THE EQUAL OF JUDGE DOUGLAS, AND THE EQUAL OF EVERY LIVING MAN.

In 1859, a Kansas vigilante named John Brown attempted to raise a slave rebellion and seize the federal arsenal at Harper's Ferry, Virginia. He was captured by U.S. Army Lieutenant Colonel Robert E. Lee, and hanged on December 2.

"I, John Brown, am now quite certain that the crimes of this guilty land will never be purged away but with blood. I had, as I now think, vainly flattered myself that without very much bloodshed it might be done."

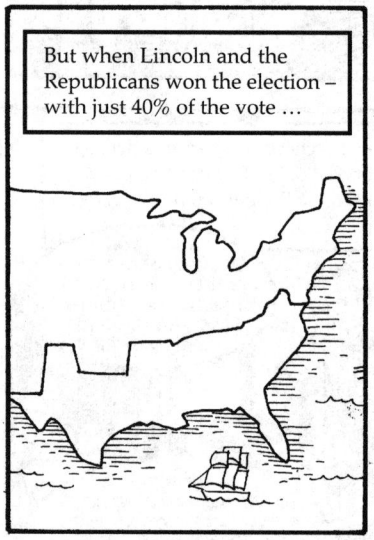

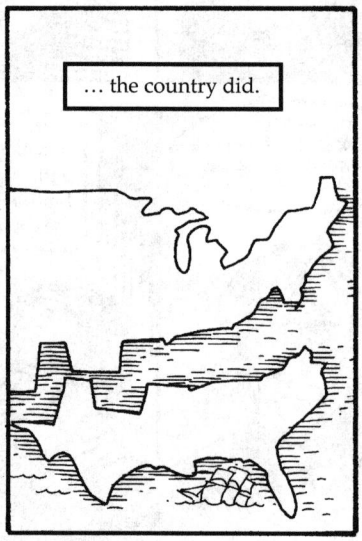

On April 12, 1861, Confederate forces fired on the U.S. flag. Fort Sumter fell, and Lincoln called for 75,000 men to put down the rebellion. He figured it might take as long as three months.

"Both parties deprecated war, but one of them would make war rather than let the nation survive, and the other would accept war rather than let it perish, and the war came."

So the job went to Irvin McDowell, who had never commanded troops in combat, but was a friend of the secretary of the Treasury.

He did pretty well at Manassas ...

... until the Virginians showed up, and General "Stonewall" Jackson got his nickname.
THERE STANDS JACKSON LIKE A STONE WALL! RALLY BEHIND THE VIRGINIANS!

So McDowell was out and George McClellan took over.
YOU MAY CALL ME "THE YOUNG NAPOLEON."

It took McClellan ten months to bring the Confederate army to battle.

It took Lee and Jackson seven days to beat him.

Things went better at sea. The Union Navy blockaded the Confederacy's coast and cut off Southern trade.

ANY O' Y'ALL WANNA BUY SOME COTTON?

And in Tennessee the Navy and the Army wiped out two Confederate forts, and took Nashville. The North had at least one good general.

NO TERMS EXCEPT *UNCONDITIONAL SURRENDER.*
Ulysses S. Grant had failed as a farmer, a shop clerk, an engineer, and a businessman. He literally could not sell ice in the summer. (It melted.)

But he could win battles.

At Shiloh, the Confederates had total surprise. Half of Grant's troops were raw recruits, and Grant's subordinate General Lew Wallace spent one entire day marching in circles instead of attacking.

WHAT DOES HE THINK THIS IS? A *CHARIOT* RACE?

Grant still won.

NOW, HERE'S THE PLAN. TO BEAT MCCLELLAN, WE'LL SPLIT INTO FOUR PARTS, PIN OURSELVES AGAINST THE RIVER, AND LOSE OUR CAVALRY SOMEWHERE.

YOU'RE A TRUE GENTLEMAN, MARSE ROBERT.

IT'S ONLY FAIR.

Meanwhile, back East, Robert E. Lee was invading the Union.

McClellan even found a copy of Lee's battle plans wrapped around a cigar.

MMMM ... GENIUS-Y ...

So at Antietam, McClellan managed a draw. Lee had to march back south.

I STILL THINK YOUR "TIES GO TO THE UNION" RULE IS A LITTLE TOO SPORTING.

FAIR'S FAIR.

But a draw was close enough for Lincoln to issue the Emancipation Proclamation five days later.

I HEREBY PROCLAIM ALL THE SLAVES IN REBEL TERRITORY FREED.

ONCE GRANT CAN GET THERE TO ACTUALLY FREE THEM.

"My paramount object in this struggle is to save the Union, and is not either to save or to destroy slavery. if I could save the Union without freeing any slave I would do it, and if I could save it by freeing all the slaves I would do it; and if I could save it by freeing some and leaving others alone I would also do that."

I TOLD YOU, I THOUGHT HE WUZ A *YANKEE GENERAL!*
YOU IDJIT! HE AIN'T A YANKEE GENERAL, HE'S A *WINNING* GENERAL!
Slowly, the tide turned for the Union. The South won at Chancellorsville the next year, but his own men accidentally shot Stonewall Jackson, who died a week later.

Cutting the South in two, and taking the entire Mississippi River valley for the Union, Grant celebrated July Fourth in 1863 by taking Vicksburg.

Lee spent the day before losing the Battle of Gettysburg.
IT IS MY FAULT. IT IS ALL MY FAULT.

It was the bloodiest battle of the war: over 27,000 wounded, and almost 8,000 dead.

Lincoln made sure they didn't die in vain.

The North used black troops. The South wouldn't. The North had a million immigrants during the war. The South had a blockaded coastline.

In 1864, Grant put his friend William Tecumseh Sherman in charge of bringing modern war to the Deep South.
YOU CANNOT QUALIFY WAR IN HARSHER TERMS THAN I WILL. WAR IS CRUELTY, AND YOU CANNOT REFINE IT; AND THOSE WHO BROUGHT WAR INTO OUR COUNTRY DESERVE ALL THE CURSES AND MALEDICTIONS A PEOPLE CAN POUR OUT.
While Grant tried to bring the fight to Robert E. Lee.
Grant steadily forced Lee southward – but at a steadily rising price.
The Democrats, at least, were tired of paying that price. They proposed an armistice at their 1864 convention, and nominated General McClellan as their candidate for president.
DON'T YOU THINK IT SENDS KIND OF A MIXED MESSAGE?
WHO HAS MORE EXPERIENCE NOT FIGHTING THE CIVIL WAR THAN HE DOES?
STOP THE WAR
McCLELLAN FOR PRESIDENT
THE UNION IS THE ONE CONDITION OF PEACE. WE ASK NO MORE.
To his credit, McClellan was as slow to fight for surrender as he was to fight for victory.
Then Sherman took Atlanta.
And General Sheridan cleared out the Shenandoah Valley.
THREE GOOD YANKEE GENERALS? UNFAIR!
DAILY BLAB
LANDSLIDE FOR LINCOLN
DEMS WIN ONLY 3
And the voters decided they weren't quite ready to quit just yet.
The soldiers weren't, either – over 70% of the army voted for Lincoln.

Sherman kept marching through Georgia, reached the sea, and then turned north into South Carolina.
Grant just kept the pressure on. When Sheridan's men joined Grant's forces in March, Lee was caught in a trap. He surrendered at Appomattox Court House on April 9, 1865.
The Civil War was over. 600,000 men were dead. And the South had lost.

And at the Precise Moment,
I, John Wilkes Booth
Valiantly Slay the Presidential Ogre...
But John Wilkes Booth, America's most famous actor, had a plan to reverse the defeat.
... LEWIS WILL REPAY SEWARD IN BLOOD, AND GEORGE WILL HEROICALLY ASSASSINATE VICE PRESIDENT JOHNSON. AND THUS INSPIRED, THE SOUTH SHALL RISE AGAIN!
SIC SEMPER
OWWW
TYRANNIS!
SWAPT
It didn't work out that way.
HOW ABOUT THAT? THIS NECK BRACE WAS GOOD FOR MY HEALTH!
Lewis Powell botched the killing of Seward.
LEMME TELL YA, SHOME ONE HIC OUGHTA KILL THE VISHE PREZDET HIC
KEEP IT DOWN, MAC. YOU'LL WAKE HIM UP.
Instead of killing Johnson, George Atzerodt just got drunk and wandered off.
The Confederacy still died in flames.
POW!
So did Booth.
And Abraham Lincoln belonged to the ages.

PART THREE

YEARNING TO BREATHE FREE *1865-1898*

"Give me your tired, your poor,
Your huddled masses yearning to breathe free,
The wretched refuse of your teeming shore.
Send these, the homeless, tempest-tost to me,
I lift my lamp beside the golden door!"
— from "The New Colossus," by Emma Lazarus

With the slave-owning South out of Congress during the Civil War, Western Republicans could finally pass the Homestead Act in 1862. Any farmer who settled on 160 acres of land could claim it, free of charge, after five years. The government eventually gave away 10% of all the land in the United States to homesteaders.
After the Civil War, Texas ranchers could once more sell their beef in the hungry North. Cowboys drove the cattle north from Texas along the Chisholm Trail to the Kansas railheads at Abilene, Dodge City, and Topeka.
WELCOME TO FLAVOR COUNTRY.
ON THE BRIGHT SIDE, IT'S NOW THE GOLDEN AGE OF THE GUNFIGHTER!
This golden age of the cowboy lasted until 1885, when the stock ranchers of the Texas Panhandle extended barbed wire fences across the entire open range. Range wars flared for the next decade all across the West.

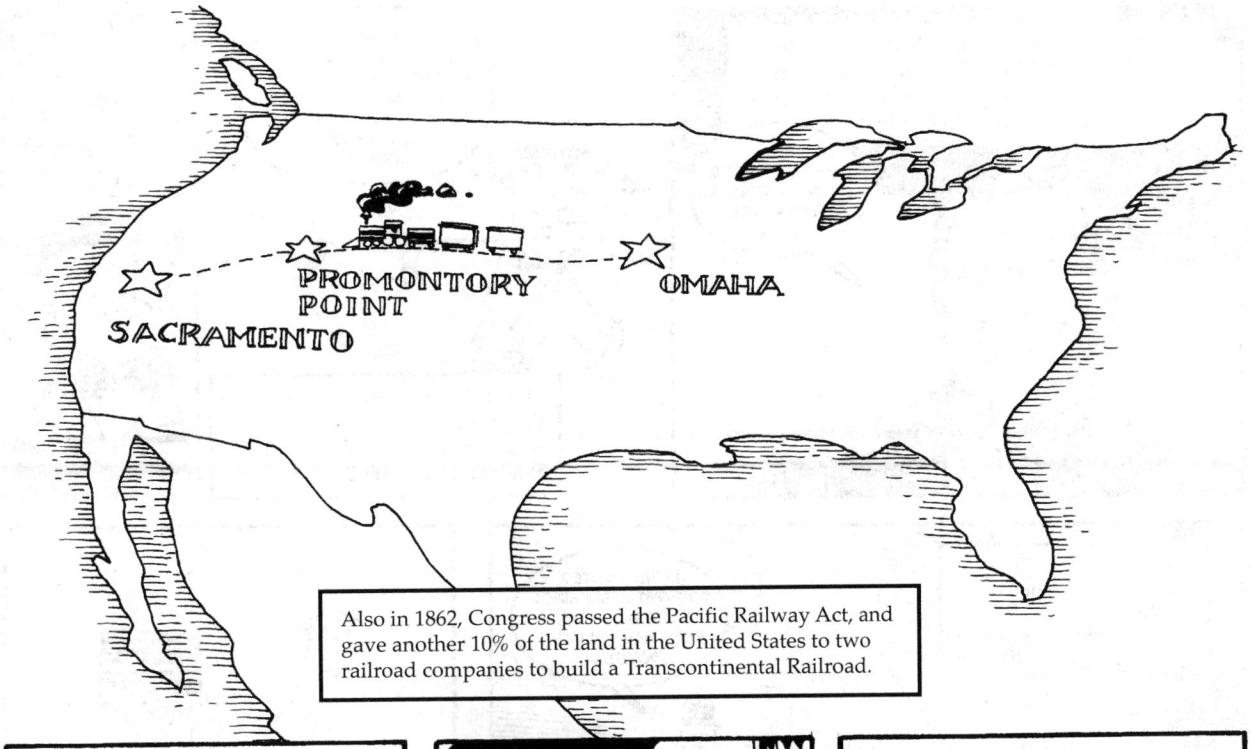

Also in 1862, Congress passed the Pacific Railway Act, and gave another 10% of the land in the United States to two railroad companies to build a Transcontinental Railroad.

The Central Pacific hired 11,000 Chinese laborers because it could pay them a third of what whites earned. The workers went on strike twice; by the time the track reached Nevada, Chinese and white pay was the same.

The two lines met on May 10, 1869, at Promontory Point, Utah. Leland Stanford drove in the final golden spike – though Chinese workers laid the last mile of track.

In 18 months in 1867-1868, "Buffalo Bill" Cody killed 4,200 bison to feed workers on the Kansas Pacific Railroad. In 1872, he formed a touring show and became America's first national celebrity.

Lincoln's assassination made his vice president, Andrew Johnson, the 17th president. Johnson was a pro-Union Democrat from Tennessee, and everything seemed to go well at first.
A LOYAL NEGRO IS MORE WORTHY THAN A DISLOYAL WHITE MAN.
THE GREAT STATE OF ALABAMA PROUDLY RATIFIES THE THIRTEENTH AMENDMENT, MAKIN' IT PART OF OUAH MAGNIFICENT CONSTI ...
... IT SAYS WHAT?
The Thirteenth Amendment to the Constitution, abolishing slavery, was ratified by two-thirds of the states on December 2, 1865.
Secretary of State Seward muscled the French out of Mexico ...
IF WE WANTED TO FIGHT A SUPERIOR INDUSTRIAL POWER, WE'D HAVE INVADED PRUSSIA!
... and bought the Russians out of Alaska.
TO REJOIN THE UNION, YOU NEED TO RATIFY THE THIRTEENTH AMENDMENT AND REPUDIATE CONFEDERATE DEBTS, AND TEN PERCENT OF YOUR VOTERS MUST SWEAR ALLEGIANCE TO THE UNION.
THAT SOUNDS EASY ENOUGH.
IT'S WHAT ABRAHAM LINCOLN WOULD HAVE WANTED.
WELL, WE'LL DO IT ANYWAY.
Johnson imposed minimal "reconstruction" requirements on the Southern states, and declared the Confederate rebellion over.

In the South, the new state governments rapidly set about passing "Black Codes" to restrict the freed slaves.
NEGROES ARE HEREBY PROHIBITED FROM OWNING BUSINESSES, TESTIFYING IN COURT, TRAVELING WITHOUT WHITE PERMISSION, WORKING IN A NON-FARM CAPACITY, OR RESISTING THESE LAWS ON PENALTY OF FORCED LABOR.
OLD TIMES HERE REALLY AREN'T FORGOTTEN!

During the war, General Sherman had confiscated some plantations and divided them among former slaves, granting "40 acres and a mule" to each free black farmer.
AND ALL THE CHARCOAL I CAN CARRY!

In September of 1865, Johnson rescinded Sherman's order, rousing Republican ire. In 1866 Congress began their own program of Reconstruction, and Johnson began his program of thwarting Congress …
WE SHALL EXTEND THE *FREEDMEN'S BUREAU* AND RESUME LAND GRANTS!
VETO!
WE SHALL PASS A *CIVIL RIGHTS BILL!*
VETO!
… and then his program of having his vetoes overridden.

(Although somehow the land grants got left out the second time around.)
I SWEAR I HAD A MULE IN HERE SOMEWHERE…

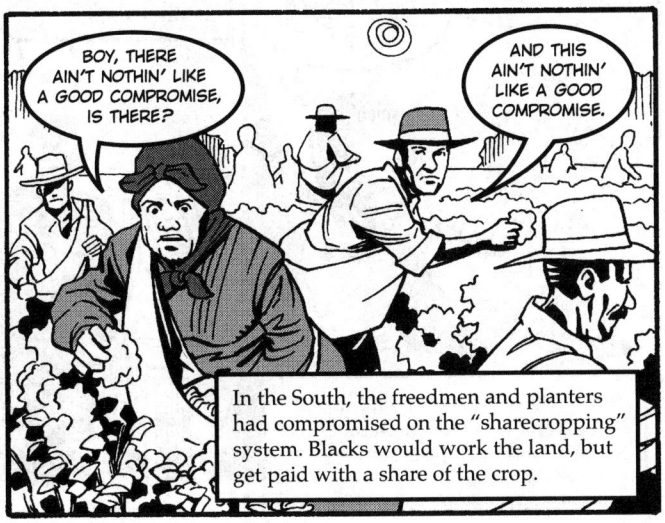
BOY, THERE AIN'T NOTHIN' LIKE A GOOD COMPROMISE, IS THERE?
AND THIS AIN'T NOTHIN' LIKE A GOOD COMPROMISE.
In the South, the freedmen and planters had compromised on the "sharecropping" system. Blacks would work the land, but get paid with a share of the crop.

In December 1865, former Confederates founded the Ku Klux Klan to terrorize blacks into subservience, committing a murder a day in some states. In the summer of 1866, race riots broke out in Memphis and New Orleans, killing over 80 blacks.
All persons born or naturalized in the United States, and subject to the jurisdiction thereof, are citizens of the United States and of the State wherein they reside. No State shall make or enforce any law which shall abridge the privileges or immunities of citizens of the United States; nor shall any State deprive any person of life, liberty, or property, without due process of law; nor deny to any person within its jurisdiction the equal protection of the laws.
Congress responded with the Fourteenth Amendment …
… and voters responded with an increased Republican majority. Radical Reconstruction was now in full swing. Congress sent the army in to occupy the South once more, supporting state governments elected by blacks and poor whites.
THIS WAS A LOT MORE FUN WHEN WE GOT TO BURN EVERYTHING.
YOUR NEGRO LEGISLATORS ARE BOUGHT BY NORTHERN RAILROAD MONEY!
SEE? A BLACK MAN CAN GOVERN JUST LIKE A WHITE ONE!
The new governments built public schools and railroads throughout the South … and took the customary piece of the action.
And they elected 17 blacks to Congress, beginning with Senator Hiram Revels – elected to fill Jefferson Davis' old seat in Mississippi.
WELL, AT LEAST HE'S A REPUBLICAN.
WHAT IS HE BEING IMPEACHED FOR, AGAIN?
FIRING HIS OWN SECRETARY OF WAR.
NO, SERIOUSLY.
Congress, meanwhile, impeached President Johnson … who got off by one vote.

Maybe 1869 would be a new beginning. Professional baseball …
19 AND 0 FOR THE YEAR!
THEY'LL JUST BREAK YOUR HEART IF YOU START CARING NOW.
… and college football both began that year, after all.
OUR RUSHING GAME WILL REALLY IMPROVE ONCE RUSHING BECOMES LEGAL.
Better yet (at least if you were black or Republican) Ulysses S. Grant was inaugurated president after winning a convincing electoral victory in 1868.
I KNOW NO METHOD TO SECURE THE REPEAL OF BAD OR OBNOXIOUS LAWS SO EFFECTIVE AS THEIR STRINGENT EXECUTION.
Grant ordered the army to crush the KKK.
NO FAIR! WE'RE NOT USED TO PEOPLE FIGHTING BACK!
The right of citizens of the United States to vote shall not be denied or abridged by the United States or by any State on account of race, color, or previous condition of servitude.
HISSS!
BOO!
And the Fifteenth Amendment was ratified in 1870, though not without opposition …

... from women's rights groups.
WHY SHOULD BLACK MEN VOTE WHEN WOMEN CANNOT?
WHEN WOMEN BECAUSE THEY ARE WOMEN ARE DRAGGED FROM THEIR HOMES AND HUNG UPON LAMP POSTS, THEN THEY WILL HAVE THE URGENCY TO OBTAIN THE BALLOT.
Women (including Susan B. Anthony) were in the forefront of the temperance movement ...
WOMEN'S CHRISTIAN TEMPERANCE UNION
IF THERE'S ANYTHING WORSE THAN A MAN CONTROLLING YOUR PROPERTY ...
... IT'S A DRUNKEN MAN CONTROLLING YOUR PROPERTY.
... and the labor reform movement.
WORKING WOMEN'S PROTECTIVE UNION
IF THERE'S ANYTHING WORSE THAN WORKING CONDITIONS TODAY ...
... IT'S WORKING CONDITIONS FOR WOMEN TODAY.
Women weren't the only ones feeling their oats.
I'M FEELIN' MY OATS! AND MY WHEAT! AND MY CORN!
The farmers were mad at the railroads.
OVERCHARGING FOR SHORT HAULS!
DEPOT FEES FOR THEIR ELEVATORS!
HIGH PRICES IN DROUGHT YEARS!
So beginning in 1869, they joined forces in the Grange movement, and got the states (or the states with a lot of farmers) to regulate railroad rates.
THIS CAN'T END WELL.

Railway moguls weren't the only "robber barons" of the Gilded Age. Andrew Carnegie began as an impoverished Scottish immigrant.
WE PREFER THE TERM "CAPTAINS OF INDUSTRY."

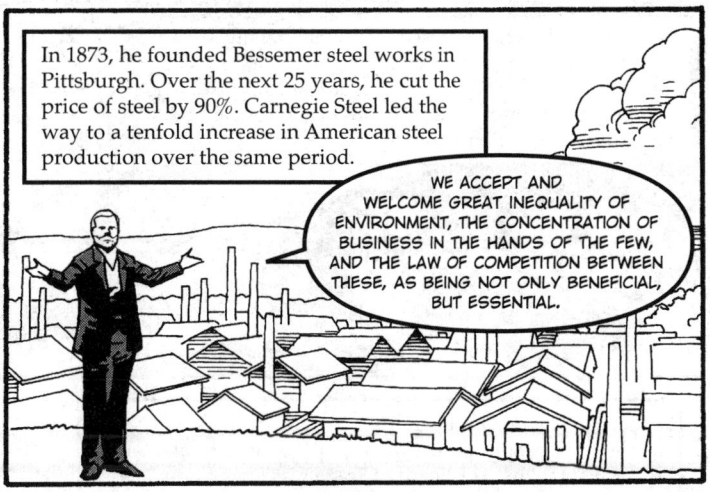
In 1873, he founded Bessemer steel works in Pittsburgh. Over the next 25 years, he cut the price of steel by 90%. Carnegie Steel led the way to a tenfold increase in American steel production over the same period.
WE ACCEPT AND WELCOME GREAT INEQUALITY OF ENVIRONMENT, THE CONCENTRATION OF BUSINESS IN THE HANDS OF THE FEW, AND THE LAW OF COMPETITION BETWEEN THESE, AS BEING NOT ONLY BENEFICIAL, BUT ESSENTIAL.

The first oil strike in America was at Titusville, Pennsylvania, in 1859. Eight years later, John D. Rockefeller, the son of a traveling salesman, put together the refinery combine that would become Standard Oil.

I BELIEVE IT IS MY DUTY TO MAKE MONEY AND STILL MORE MONEY AND TO USE THE MONEY I MAKE FOR THE GOOD OF MY FELLOW MAN ACCORDING TO THE DICTATES OF MY CONSCIENCE.
American oil production went from 2.5 million barrels in 1865 to 63 million barrels in 1900 – and Rockefeller controlled 85% of it. He also cut kerosene prices by 75% – and suddenly America could afford to read at night.

MONEY EQUALS BUSINESS WHICH EQUALS POWER, ALL OF WHICH COME FROM CHARACTER AND TRUST.
In 1869, the banker J.P. Morgan broke the control of Jay Gould and Jim Fisk over the Albany & Susquehanna Railroad, helping force New York Stock Exchange consolidation and self-regulation to prevent "stock watering."
His "Morganization" of other railroads rationalized routes and rates, improved the lines' solvency – and made Morgan rich and connected enough to refinance the entire army budget in 1877.

Railroads and money intersected almost literally in Chicago, which in 1865 created the world's first futures market, the Chicago Board of Trade. By 1870, the Chicago futures market purchased and sold about a quarter of the nation's grain.
BUY!
SELL!
DOES ANYONE ELSE SMELL SMOKE?
The next year, on October 8, 1871, the Great Fire hit Chicago. It killed 300 people, burnt down a third of the city, and left 100,000 homeless. The Board of Trade was open for business again two weeks later.
WE USE EVERYTHING BUT THE SQUEAL.
The fire missed Chicago's Union Stockyards, where rival meat-packing kings Gustavus Swift and Philip Armour invented the "disassembly line" to turn cattle and hogs into meat – and into soap, glue, fertilizer, hairbrushes, buttons, knife-handles, and insulin.
It's probably best not to wonder what went into America's first hot dogs, a snack pioneered on Coney Island in 1871.
By 1882, Swift and Armour had perfected the refrigerated train car. Chicago beef could reach Eastern cities already dressed, cheaper than the neighborhood butcher could sell it. The supermarket was now possible.

Since everybody knew that Grant would be re-elected in 1872, the big excitement was the candidacy of Victoria Woodhull, a stockbroker, spiritualist, and free-love advocate. She ran on the Equal Rights Party ticket with Frederick Douglass, and got perhaps 2,000 votes nationwide.
Susan B. Anthony voted for President Grant. She was arrested, convicted in circuit court without benefit of jury, and refused to pay her $100 fine.
IT WAS WE, THE PEOPLE; NOT WE, THE WHITE MALE CITIZENS; NOR YET WE, THE MALE CITIZENS; BUT WE, THE WHOLE PEOPLE, WHO FORMED THE UNION.
AND WE FORMED IT, NOT TO GIVE THE BLESSINGS OF LIBERTY, BUT TO SECURE THEM; NOT TO THE HALF OF OURSELVES AND THE HALF OF OUR POSTERITY, BUT TO THE WHOLE PEOPLE -- WOMEN AS WELL AS MEN.
Just like Congress! The construction company for the Union Pacific Railroad, Credit Mobilier, bribed 30 members of Congress (including both of Grant's vice presidents and the future president James Garfield) with shares in exchange for voting higher subsidies to the railroad. Two members were censured.
I'M EMBARRASSED TO ASSOCIATE WITH YOU, YOU PACK OF THIEVES.
Grant's private secretary was embezzling liquor taxes, the secretary of the Treasury was hiring tax farmers, the secretary of War was taking bribes from Indian agents, a U.S. attorney committed forgery, and the ambassador to Britain was selling phony mining stock.
AND PEOPLE SAY THE GOVERNMENT SHOULD REGULATE *MY* DEALINGS!
And when the over-inflated economy crashed in 1873, the Democrats regained control of the House for the first time since the Civil War.
PANIC!
SELL!
AAAACK!
CLOSE THE BANK!
IT'S THE *PANIC* OF *1873!* WHY AREN'T YOU PANICKING?
IT'S GOING TO LAST SIX YEARS, SO I'M PACING MYSELF.

The Panic of 1873 was the first to spread in real time all over the financial world, thanks to Morse's telegraph and the stock ticker invented by Thomas Edison in 1869.
ALL HOPE ABANDON
The holder of 1,093 patents by the time he died in 1931, Edison combined genius, celebrity, and industry like no American since Benjamin Franklin. (Edison preferred Thomas Paine, however.) His list of iconic inventions is familiar to all.
NONE OF MY INVENTIONS CAME BY ACCIDENT. I SEE A WORTHWHILE NEED TO BE MET AND I MAKE TRIAL AFTER TRIAL UNTIL IT COMES.
WHAT IT BOILS DOWN TO IS 1% INSPIRATION AND 99% PERSPIRATION.
Incandescent Lamp (1879)
The Mimeograph (1876)
Phonograph (1877)
In 1882, Edison also created the first electrical power plant in the world, for New York City street lighting.
SO, MR. EDISON, I'VE WORKED OUT THE INTERMITTENT SHUTTER, THE SPROCKETS, AND THE OPTICS. I THINK THIS CAMERA WILL ACTUALLY CAPTURE MOVING PICTURES!
WONDERFUL! WE'LL CALL IT THE EDISON KINETOGRAPH!
CATCHY NAME, SIR.
In 1876 at Menlo Park, New Jersey, Edison created perhaps his most significant invention – the industrial research laboratory. By combining his vision, the abilities of scores of assistants, and ample resources, Edison applied mass production to the process of invention.

The United States of America celebrated its Centennial in 1876 at a grand Exhibition in Philadelphia. Like other Victorian-era World's Fairs, it included demonstrations of new inventions, including Edison's quadruplex telegraph.
Sholes and Glidden Remington typewriter
George Westinghouse's air brake
The Otis Company's steam elevator
The Emperor of Brazil received a demonstration of Alexander Graham Bell's new telephone.
QUEM E WATSON?

The election of 1876 pitted the reforming governor of New York, Samuel J. Tilden, against the most honest man the Republicans could find, Civil War hero and governor of Ohio Rutherford B. Hayes.
I BROKE BOSS TWEED!
I HAVE A VERY IMPRESSIVE BEARD. MY OPPONENT HAS NO BEARD WHATSOEVER.
AS AN INCREDIBLY RICH NEW YORK LAWYER, I KNOW CORRUPTION WHEN I SEE IT.
I WOULD NOT KNOW, AS I SPENT THE WAR YEARS BEING SHOT FOUR TIMES BY DEMOCRATIC TRAITORS!!!
The Democrats crusaded against Republican corruption. The Republicans responded by "waving the bloody shirt" of the Civil War.
Although Tilden won the popular vote by 150,000 votes, three occupied Southern states turned in disputed ballots. So Congress appointed a 15-man commission – 8 Republicans and 7 Democrats – to settle the question. So guess who won?
THE REPUBLICAN GOVERNOR CHEATED!
I'M GLAD WE'LL NEVER HAVE TO GO THROUGH ANYTHING LIKE THIS AGAIN.
COUNTY OFFICIALS SUPPRESSED THE BLACK VOTE IN FLORIDA!
The Democrats agreed to take a dive if Hayes would withdraw federal troops from the South and end Reconstruction. Hayes took the Presidency; the Democrats took the South back.
I BET I KNOW WHO LOST.

In 1874, Lt. Col. George Armstrong Custer discovered gold on Sioux tribal land in the Black Hills of South Dakota, and set off a gold rush of Americans panicked (and impoverished) by the Crash of 1873. Led by the shaman Sitting Bull and the warriors Gall and Crazy Horse, approximately 25,000 Sioux left the reservation.
THESE HILLS ARE SACRED TO US!
WELL, SINCE LAST YEAR, THEY'RE HOLY TO US TOO!

General George Crook set out to crush the Sioux. On June 25, 1876, Crook's subordinate Custer led his 7th Cavalry in a rash attack on a Sioux village on the Little Bighorn River.
The Sioux obliterated Custer's entire command, and the 7th Cavalry as a whole suffered 52% casualties. Sitting Bull, Gall, and a handful of Sioux escaped into Canada that winter; the U.S. Army forced the rest back onto the reservation in 1877.

In 1877, rather than go onto the reservation, Chief Joseph led 800 Nez Perce on a four-month fighting retreat toward Canada. He was intercepted by General Nelson Miles less than 40 miles from the border and surrendered on October 5.
HEAR ME, MY CHIEFS! I AM TIRED; MY HEART IS SICK AND SAD. FROM WHERE THE SUN NOW STANDS, I WILL FIGHT NO MORE FOREVER.

The last great Indian war leader, the Apache chief Geronimo, surrendered to General Miles in September 1886. He and 38 warriors had eluded 5,000 men – a quarter of the U.S. Army – for over a year. The army had been fighting the Apaches almost continuously since 1862.
I CAN'T BELIEVE YOU ACTUALLY WANTED THIS LAND.
On January 1, 1889, a Paiute shaman named Wovoka witnessed a solar eclipse, and announced he had a vision of a future paradise, achievable by performing the Ghost Dance. In 1890, the Ghost Dance movement spread to the Sioux reservation, where it panicked the U.S. Army into a massacre of 200 Sioux at Wounded Knee Creek.
Some of the tribes settled in Oklahoma had fought for the Confederacy, so the government confiscated their land after the Civil War. At high noon on April 22, 1889, 50,000 people raced into the former Indian Territory for the last good homestead land in the West.
WHAT ARE YOU DOING HERE?
I JUST DECIDED TO SNEAK IN A LITTLE SOONER, IS ALL.
PRIVATE PROPERTY
WHY, THAT'S STEALING! STEALING INDIAN TERRITORY IS ... UNNATURAL!
The next year, the Superintendent of the Census announced that "there could hardly be said to be a frontier line" remaining in the West.

By 1877, the Panic of 1873 had turned into full-fledged depression. A quarter of the railroads were out of business, and unemployment was 15%. Many who still had jobs worked half the year or less.
YOU HEAR ABOUT CUSTER? KILLED BY INJUNS BEFORE HE KNEW WHAT HIT 'IM.
LUCKY BASTARD.
On July 14, B&O Railroad workers in Martinsburg, West Virginia, learned they would be getting their second pay cut in two months. They went on strike instead, preventing trains from running on the fourth-largest railroad in the United States.
The strike spread across the Midwest – the strikers controlled the railroads and telegraph stations. Governors ordered out state militias; some fired on strikers, while others joined them. 80,000 workers were on strike across the country; half the railroad traffic in the nation was halted.
MARTINSBURG
MILWAUKEE
PITTSBURGH
ST. LOUIS
LEBANON
ALTOONA
CLEVELAND
BALTIMORE
PHILADELPHIA
BLOOMINGTON
URBANA
COLUMBUS
CHICAGO
NEWARK
CINCINNATI
DECATUR
NEW YORK
STRIKE!
BUFFALO
LOUISVILLE
PEORIA
READING
In St. Louis, strikers shut down the whole city in a general strike. For two or three days, revolution was in the air again.
ALL YOU HAVE TO DO, GENTLEMEN, FOR YOU HAVE THE NUMBERS, IS TO UNITE ON ONE IDEA -- THAT THE WORKINGMEN SHALL RULE THE COUNTRY.
WHAT MAN MAKES, BELONGS TO HIM, AND THE WORKINGMEN MADE THIS COUNTRY.
In late July, President Hayes ordered out federal troops. They shot no one, in many cases appearing after strike enthusiasm had waned – or been choked by "the rifle diet." Police and militia had killed 100 people, and thousands were jailed and fired.

I'LL TELL YOU WHAT CAUSED THE STRIKE! IT'S ALL THOSE GERMANS!
EVERYBODY KNOWS THE GERMANS ARE SLOPPY, UNDISCIPLINED, LAZY, GOOD-FOR-NOTHINGS!
Looking for someone to blame, many Americans pointed the finger at the new breed of foreigner. Although Irish and English still flooded in between 1870 and 1890, neither group equaled the 2 million German immigrants during that period.
This wave of Germans brought two signature contributions to American life. One caught on immediately.
SAY, PARTNER, WHAT DO YOU CALL THAT?
EIN HAMBURGER-SANDVICH.
The other one didn't.
SAY, PARTNER, WHAT'RE YOU READING, THERE?
SOCIALISM.
KARL MARX
KARL MARX
I HAVE ALL EIGHT DAILY AMERICAN SOCIALIST NEWSPAPERS -- IN GERMAN!
NEWS
THERE ARE AT LEAST THREE THINGS WRONG WITH YOUR MARKETING PLAN.
Germany clamped down on socialists – who fled to America. In 1876, America's first socialist party, the Workingmen's Party, had only 3,000 members, mostly Germans. They had excellent organizational skills, though – Workingmen's Party agitators took lead roles in the Strike of 1877 …
… and in the Chinese Exclusion movement. Dennis Kearney, an Irish immigrant, headed the Workingmen's Party in San Francisco, and lobbied ceaselessly against "coolie labor," winning support from white workers nationwide.
EIGHT HOUR DAY
THE CHINESE MUST GO!
CHINESE CHEAP LABOR IS A CURSE TO OUR LAND, A MENACE TO OUR LIBERTIES AND THE INSTITUTIONS OF OUR COUNTRY AND SHOULD BE RESTRICTED AND FOREVER ABOLISHED!
IRISH CHEAP LABOR, ON THE OTHER HAND …
IF ONLY WE'D THOUGHT OF THAT.
President Hayes signed the Exclusion Treaty with China in 1880. Congress ended Chinese immigration two years later, the first significant restriction on immigration in American history.

The Republicans replaced the now-tainted Hayes with the then-tainted James A. Garfield, who won a narrow victory in 1880.
In May of 1881, President Garfield promised his support to Clara Barton, who founded an American branch of the International Red Cross.
I FORESEE AN EMERGENCY OF A MEDICAL NATURE.
Garfield served one more month until he was shot by a deranged job-seeker.
MAKE ME AMBASSADOR TO AUSTRIA! OR FRANCE. FRANCE WOULD BE GOOD.
Not coincidentally, Garfield's successor, Chester A. Arthur, signed the Pendleton Act, which set down new rules for political job-seeking.
RULE ONE: NO SHOOTING THE PRESIDENT.
Meanwhile, disgruntled job-holders were building ever larger national unions. The Knights of Labor, founded in 1867, resembled Freemasonry. Samuel Gompers' Federation of Organized Trades and Labor Unions – which became the American Federation of Labor in 1886 – resembled a tidal wave.
THERE IS NOT A RIGHT TOO LONG DENIED TO WHICH WE DO NOT ASPIRE IN ORDER TO ACHIEVE; THERE IS NOT A WRONG TOO LONG ENDURED THAT WE ARE NOT DETERMINED TO ABOLISH.
SECURITY IN OUR JOBS
NO IMMIGRANT LABOR
A FAIR DAY'S PAY FOR A FAIR DAY'S WORK
BOYCOTT UNFAIR FIRMS

In 1884, the Democrats nominated Grover Cleveland for president. He was an admitted adulterer and draft-dodger ...
MA, MA, WHERE'S MY PA?
GONE TO THE WHITE HOUSE, HA HA HA!
... but he was ruthlessly principled and honest. Cleveland squeaked into office as the first Democratic President since James Buchanan.
During Cleveland's first term, the "Eight-Hour Day" movement picked up steam, and the occasional brick.
EIGHT HOUR DAY
NO SCABS
The movement's center was Chicago, with its 300,000 German workers, who included plenty of socialists, anarchists, and other radicals. To support the Eight-Hour Day, Chicago workers called a general strike on May 1, 1886.
MAY DAY!!!
MAYDAY!
On May 4, a bomb exploded at an anarchist rally in Chicago's Haymarket Square, killing a policeman. In the ensuing riot, 7 policemen and 4 workers were killed.
Nobody knew who threw the bomb, but a Chicago court convicted eight German anarchist activists – three of whom were not even at the rally – of conspiracy anyway. Governor Altgeld pardoned the surviving three in 1892, calling the entire affair "a miscarriage of justice."
THE TIME WILL COME WHEN OUR SILENCE WILL BE MORE POWERFUL THAN THE VOICES YOU STRANGLE TODAY.

Chicago was booming in another sense, as well. With its old downtown destroyed by the fire, it was ground zero for a new industrial architecture combining new powered elevators with suddenly cheaper steel frames. Architect William LeBaron Jenney built the Home Insurance Building in 1884, the first "skyscraper."
FORM EVER FOLLOWS FUNCTION. THIS IS THE LAW.
With his partner, Dankmar Adler, Chicago architect Louis Sullivan designed 90 major buildings in the next decade, reshaping the sky above America's cities.
Meanwhile, Frederick Law Olmstead, the designer of New York's Central Park (completed 1873) founded the first American landscape architecture firm in 1883.
WE WANT A GROUND TO WHICH PEOPLE MAY EASILY GO AFTER THEIR DAY'S WORK IS DONE, AND WHERE THEY MAY STROLL FOR AN HOUR, SEEING, HEARING, AND FEELING NOTHING OF THE BUSTLE AND JAR OF THE STREETS, WHERE THEY SHALL, IN EFFECT, FIND THE CITY PUT FAR AWAY FROM THEM.
Olmstead collaborated with Chicago architect Daniel Burnham to design the "White City" Columbian Exposition of 1893, a World's Fair in Chicago that spread the "City Beautiful" message to cities all across the country.
MAKE NO LITTLE PLANS. THEY HAVE NO MAGIC TO STIR MEN'S BLOOD.
Burnham designed New York's first skyscraper, the Flatiron Building, in 1902, and created the first urban growth plan, the Plan of Chicago, in 1909.

Chicago's Sears, Roebuck & Company planned big. Founded in 1886 as a mail-order watch company, by 1893 Sears sold sewing machines, plows, cream separators, clothing, and labor-saving machinery by mail at rock-bottom prices. Over a decade, Sears' Catalog circulation climbed to 3 million primarily rural customers, creating a national mass market.
SEARS
MANY A SMALL THING HAS BEEN MADE LARGE BY THE RIGHT KIND OF ADVERTISING.
Mark Twain likewise sold his books by subscription and advertising; 400,000 copies by 1880. His great American novel, *Huckleberry Finn*, sold 10,000 copies a month when it was published in 1885.
Mark Twain was far from the only "national brand." From its beginnings as a patent medicine in 1886, Coca-Cola was advertised and sold in every state and territory of the Union by 1895. In 1899, Coca-Cola invented the modern franchise system by licensing bottling rights – and the right to sub-license them.
STRIKE!
PUBLICITY, PUBLICITY, PUBLICITY IS THE GREATEST MORAL FACTOR AND FORCE IN OUR PUBLIC LIFE.
SMASHES SPA
GREAT NAVAL
With mass markets came mass newspapers. Beginning in 1882, Joseph Pulitzer kept the sales price of the *New York World* low, provided sensational crime and muck-raking stories to draw mass readership, and charged mass advertisers (such as the new department stores) to pay for it.
William Randolph Hearst followed the Pulitzer pattern with his *San Francisco Examiner* in 1887, and expanded his newspaper empire to five cities by 1904, and to 20 cities by 1928. America had a mass media.
SCREAMS OF ELDERLY PATIENTS WERE QUICKLY STILLED BY FLAMES
NEWS IS SOMETHING SOMEBODY DOESN'T WANT PRINTED; ALL ELSE IS ADVERTISING

In 1888, Republican Benjamin Harrison was the first presidential candidate to make speeches on his own behalf during a campaign. A new mass politics was being born, too …
PROVIDENCE WILL ASSURE US THE VICTORY THIS NOVEMBER.
… although Harrison still won the old-fashioned way.
HERE'S YOUR VOTIN' BONUS, "PROVIDENCE."
VOTE HERE
In 1887, Congress set up the Interstate Commerce Commission, answering the Grange demands for railroad regulation … sort of.
THE COMMISSION IS, OR CAN BE MADE, OF GREAT USE TO THE RAILROADS … THE PART OF WISDOM IS NOT TO DESTROY THE COMMISSION, BUT TO UTILIZE IT.
ONE-STOP SHOPPING, AS IT WERE.
In 1890, the muckrakers won a victory when Harrison signed the Sherman Anti-Trust Act outlawing "combinations in restraint of trade"– trusts and monopolies.
BY A VOTE OF 242-0, THE SHERMAN ACT PASSES.
WE ARE STILL REPUBLICANS, RIGHT?
In 1892, the Carnegie Trust – and Carnegie's trustworthiness – took a beating when workers struck his Bessemer Works at Homestead, Pennsylvania. Carnegie's manager Henry Clay Frick attacked the strikers with gun-wielding Pinkertons, killing nine of them.
I THOUGHT CARNEGIE SAID NO STEEL MILL WAS WORTH A SINGLE DROP OF BLOOD.
I GUESS IT DEPENDS ON WHOSE BLOOD HE WAS TALKING ABOUT.
But the strikers lost sympathy when a Russian anarchist, Alexander Berkman, attempted to assassinate Frick. Carnegie broke the strike, and the union went bankrupt defending its leaders from criminal charges.
THEORETICALLY, THIS SHOULD BE GOING BETTER.

Meanwhile, the Third Great Awakening, started by Dwight Moody in Chicago in 1860, was becoming the Social Gospel.
CHRISTIANITY IS IN ITS NATURE REVOLUTIONARY.
SLUM CLEARANCE
PROHIBITION
END CHILD LABOR
EIGHT HOUR DAY
On the farms, such fervor, and constant credit shortages, helped drive the Populist movement …
RAISE LESS CORN AND MORE HELL!
… culminating in the Populist Party convention in 1892.
INITIATIVE!
SECRET BALLOT!
WHAT DO WE WANT?
REFERENDUM!
INCOME TAX!
FREE SILVER!
DIRECT ELECTION OF SENATORS!
NO IMMIGRANTS!
The Populists carried four states; President Harrison carried 12. Grover Cleveland carried 22, and won back the White House …
I DON'T KNOW WHETHER I'M COMING OR GOING.
YOU'RE GOING.
… just in time for the Depression of 1893, another inflationary crisis that bankrupted three major railroads and threw a quarter of the country out of work.
Employees of the Pullman Sleeping Car Company weren't out of work, but Pullman cut their wages without reducing the rent in their company housing. So they struck in 1894, paralyzing the railroad network.

Cleveland ordered the military to break the Pullman strike for interfering with the U.S. Mail, and filed an anti-trust injunction against the American Railway Union, calling its sympathy strike a "combination in restraint of trade."
IF IT TAKES THE ENTIRE ARMY AND NAVY OF THE UNITED STATES TO DELIVER A POSTCARD IN CHICAGO, THAT CARD WILL BE DELIVERED.
YOU'RE UNDER ARREST FOR VIOLATING THE SHERMAN ANTI-TRUST ACT.
With the strike broken, the court convicted Eugene V. Debs, head of the ARU, of violating the no-boycott injunction, and jailed him for six months.
I'M PRETTY SURE THAT'S NOT RIGHT.
YOU'LL HAVE PLENTY OF TIME TO LOOK IT UP IN JAIL, PAL.
The economic crisis also drained the government's gold reserves, which dropped from $121 million in 1893 to $9 million in February of 1895. Cleveland was forced to get J.P. Morgan to bail the Treasury out. Morgan's syndicate got U.S. gold reserves back up to $100 million by June – and made $3.5 million in profit on the transaction.
MR. MORGAN, YOU'VE SAVED THE U.S. DOLLAR!
WHICH IS A GOOD THING, AS I HAVE SO VERY MANY MORE OF THEM NOW.
Such deals drove the Democrats into a frenzy of populism. They nominated the devout William Jennings Bryan for president in 1896 on a platform of freely coined silver and renewed inflation.
WE WILL ANSWER THEIR DEMAND FOR A GOLD STANDARD BY SAYING TO THEM: YOU SHALL NOT PRESS DOWN UPON THE BROW OF LABOR THIS CROWN OF THORNS, YOU SHALL NOT CRUCIFY MANKIND UPON A CROSS OF GOLD.
The Republican nominee, William McKinley, won the votes not just of businessmen, but also Germans, factory workers, railroad workers, the middle class, and even some farmers – and the presidency.
One of McKinley's first acts was to sign a treaty annexing the "Republic" of Hawaii, a creation of sugar planters who wanted access to the U.S. market. America had taken its first irrevocable step offshore.
FROM SEA, TO SHINING SEA, TO ... WHAT?

PART FOUR

RENDEZVOUS WITH DESTINY *1898-1945*

"There is a mysterious cycle in human events. To some generations much is given. Of other generations much is expected. This generation of Americans has a rendezvous with destiny."
—Franklin Delano Roosevelt, 1936
February 15, 1898. Havana harbor.

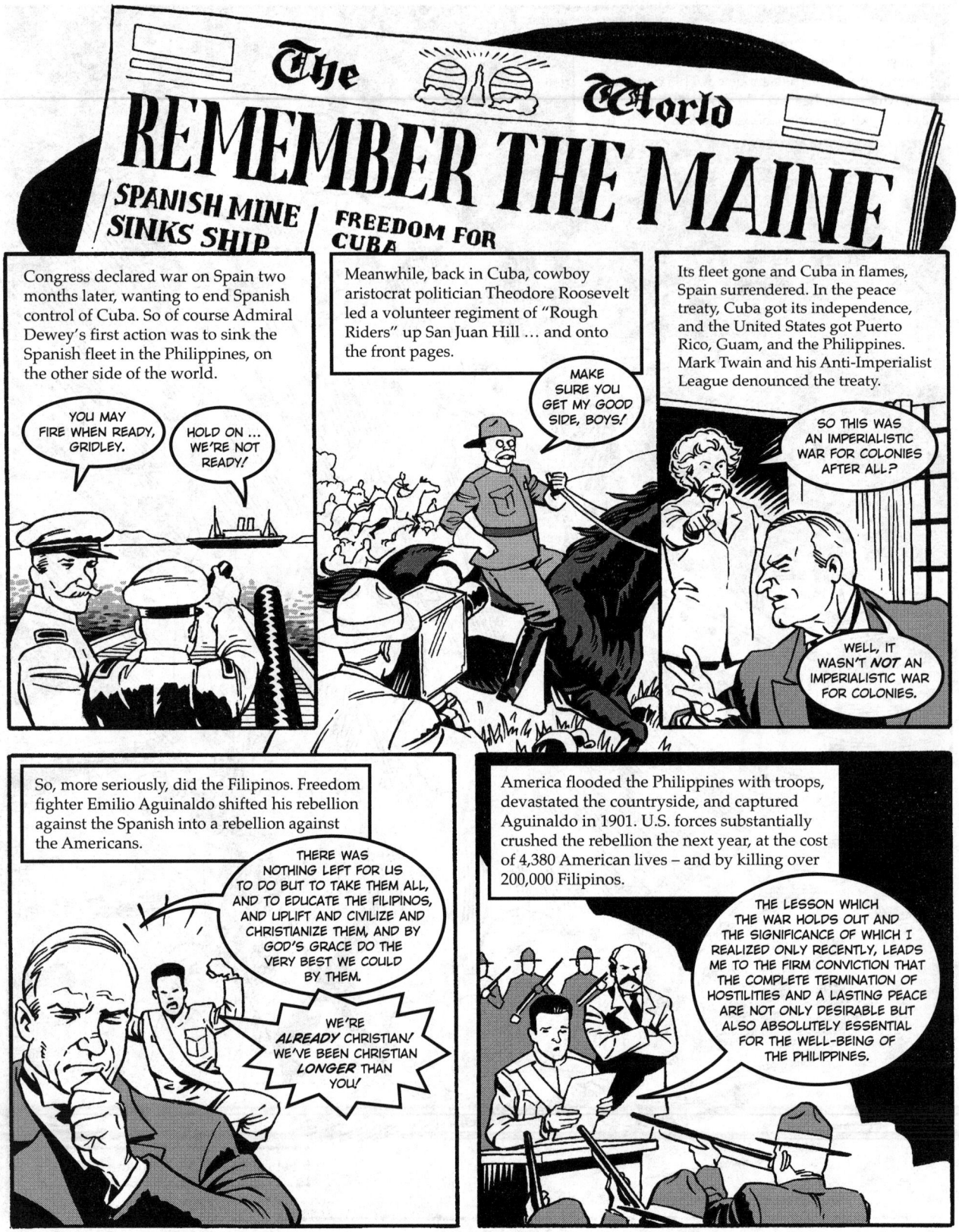
The World
REMEMBER THE MAINE
SPANISH MINE SINKS SHIP
FREEDOM FOR CUBA
Congress declared war on Spain two months later, wanting to end Spanish control of Cuba. So of course Admiral Dewey's first action was to sink the Spanish fleet in the Philippines, on the other side of the world.
YOU MAY FIRE WHEN READY, GRIDLEY.
HOLD ON ... WE'RE NOT READY!
Meanwhile, back in Cuba, cowboy aristocrat politician Theodore Roosevelt led a volunteer regiment of "Rough Riders" up San Juan Hill ... and onto the front pages.
MAKE SURE YOU GET MY GOOD SIDE, BOYS!
Its fleet gone and Cuba in flames, Spain surrendered. In the peace treaty, Cuba got its independence, and the United States got Puerto Rico, Guam, and the Philippines. Mark Twain and his Anti-Imperialist League denounced the treaty.
SO THIS WAS AN IMPERIALISTIC WAR FOR COLONIES AFTER ALL?
WELL, IT WASN'T NOT AN IMPERIALISTIC WAR FOR COLONIES.
So, more seriously, did the Filipinos. Freedom fighter Emilio Aguinaldo shifted his rebellion against the Spanish into a rebellion against the Americans.
THERE WAS NOTHING LEFT FOR US TO DO BUT TO TAKE THEM ALL, AND TO EDUCATE THE FILIPINOS, AND UPLIFT AND CIVILIZE AND CHRISTIANIZE THEM, AND BY GOD'S GRACE DO THE VERY BEST WE COULD BY THEM.
WE'RE ALREADY CHRISTIAN! WE'VE BEEN CHRISTIAN LONGER THAN YOU!
America flooded the Philippines with troops, devastated the countryside, and captured Aguinaldo in 1901. U.S. forces substantially crushed the rebellion the next year, at the cost of 4,380 American lives – and by killing over 200,000 Filipinos.
THE LESSON WHICH THE WAR HOLDS OUT AND THE SIGNIFICANCE OF WHICH I REALIZED ONLY RECENTLY, LEADS ME TO THE FIRM CONVICTION THAT THE COMPLETE TERMINATION OF HOSTILITIES AND A LASTING PEACE ARE NOT ONLY DESIRABLE BUT ALSO ABSOLUTELY ESSENTIAL FOR THE WELL-BEING OF THE PHILIPPINES.

A different sort of overwhelming power was making Buffalo, New York, America's most advanced city. In 1896, George Westinghouse harnessed Niagara Falls for hydroelectricity, using the polyphase motor invented by Nikola Tesla.

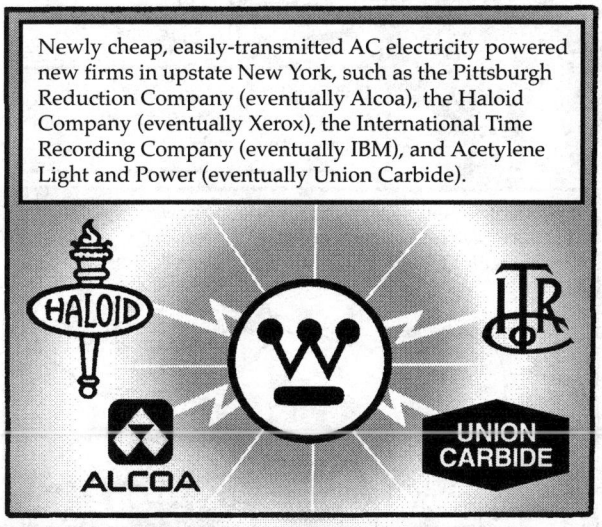
Newly cheap, easily-transmitted AC electricity powered new firms in upstate New York, such as the Pittsburgh Reduction Company (eventually Alcoa), the Haloid Company (eventually Xerox), the International Time Recording Company (eventually IBM), and Acetylene Light and Power (eventually Union Carbide).
HALOID
ALCOA
UNION CARBIDE

All of this made "The City of Light" the ideal host for the Pan-American Exposition of 1901 – where an anarchist named Leon Czolgosz shot President McKinley.

McKinley's vice president, Theodore Roosevelt, became the youngest President in American history. His "Square Deal" of trust-busting and regulation departed from McKinley's domestic policy …
NO JOB DISCRIMINATION AGAINST UNIONS!
MANDATE RAILROAD RATES!
MEAT INSPECTIONS!
PURE FOOD AND DRUG ACT!

I SPEAK SOFTLY, CARRY A BIG STICK, AND IMPROVE LATIN AMERICAN BOND RATINGS!
… but his muscular "big stick" foreign policy was McKinley on steroids. The "Roosevelt Corollary" to the Monroe Doctrine pronounced that the United States could intervene in Latin America in cases of "chronic wrongdoing or impotence."

Roosevelt's most blatant intervention came in 1903, when canal treaty negotiations with Colombia broke down.
SO, IT'S AGREED. WE CAN BUILD A CANAL THROUGH PANAMA FOR $ 10 MILLION.
DID I SAY $ 10 MILLION? I MEANT $ 20 MILLION.
FINE, $ 20 MILLION IT IS.
PLUS A $ 20 MILLION SURCHARGE.
WHERE DID I PUT MY STICK?
IN RECOGNITION OF YOUR DESPERATE ...
SIX HOURS.
... DESPERATE SIX HOURS OF STRUGGLE FOR FREEDOM, THE UNITED STATES JOYFULLY RECOGNIZES THE INDEPENDENCE OF ...
PANAMA.
... OF PANAMA AND PROMISES AMERICAN AID IN DIGGING ANY CANAL YOU MAY WISH TO SELL US.
Roosevelt created an independent Panama and negotiated a new canal treaty in two weeks.
While digging up Panama, Roosevelt moved to preserve the American West. He set aside 194 million acres of national parks and forests.
BULLY!
A similar reverence for nature infused the new "Prairie Style" of American architecture, especially that of Frank Lloyd Wright.
NO HOUSE SHOULD EVER BE ON A HILL OR ON ANYTHING. IT SHOULD BE OF THE HILL.
Nature, on the other hand, seemed downright irreverent on April 18, 1906. The earthquake and fire that hit San Francisco killed perhaps 3,000 people.

On December 17, 1903, at Kitty Hawk, North Carolina, Orville and Wilbur Wright did Nature one better. Man could fly.

The Wright Flyer was powered by gasoline. So, increasingly, was America. On January 10, 1901, an oil strike in Spindletop, Texas, tripled American oil production overnight. By the time the Wrights' Flyer III flew in 1905, the Santa Fe Railroad had gone from one oil-fired locomotive to 227.
Some 600 new oil companies sprang up in Texas alone, effectively breaking the Standard Oil monopoly. The first gas station opened in St. Louis in 1905.
With gasoline cheap and getting cheaper, a mechanic named Henry Ford took the obvious next step.
BUNK! IF IT'S SO OBVIOUS, I'D LIKE TO SEE YOU DO IT.
His Model T was easy to drive, rugged and reliable, and cheap to build. He sold the first ones in 1908 for a mere $850, a third the cost of other cars.
In 1913, he reversed the meat-packers' "disassembly line," and cut the time to build a Model T by 85%. A Model T now cost $550; sales increased twenty-fold.
With that, Ford decided to share the profits. In 1914, he established a $5 per day minimum salary (more than double the previous amount) and a 40-hour workweek for all Ford workers. His costs actually fell, and so did Model T prices – again. Sales increased by 150%.
OF COURSE IT IS NOT THE EMPLOYER WHO PAYS WAGES. HE ONLY HANDLES THE MONEY. IT IS THE PRODUCT THAT PAYS THE WAGES.

Thanks to Willis Haviland Carrier, those cars could start going south. Carrier patented his "Apparatus for Treating Air" in 1906, and began air-conditioning factories, incidentally improving the quality of paint, tobacco, film, meat, and drugs.
By 1921, Carrier had invented the "centrifugal chiller," which could air-condition large indoor spaces; by 1928, the home air conditioner was practical. Business, industry, and population could move south and create the Sun Belt.
THE PLOT ISN'T MUCH, BUT THE EFFECTS ARE TERRIFIC.
At least one industry beat the rush to the sun. Motion pictures followed D.W. Griffith to Hollywood beginning in 1910.
HAND OVER YOUR FILM, YOU PATENT-INFRINGING VARMINT!
NO SIR. YOU CAN TELL MR. EDISON I'M GOING TO CALIFORNIA!
Another American art form was emerging in the South: New Orleans jazz. By 1910, "Jelly Roll" Morton was touring the country.
Yellow-journalistic competition between Hearst and Pulitzer drove the third new American art form of the era, comics. In 1904, its first great genius, Winsor McKay, debuted in the even yellower *New York Herald*.
MY! THIS DECADE IS CERTAINLY OCCUPYING A GREAT NUMBER OF PAGES!

W.C. Handy's "Memphis Blues" in 1909 was the first major blues song to be widely performed and published. This fourth American art form of the 1900s grew from bloodstained soil.
THAT MELANCHOLY STRAIN, THAT EVER-HAUNTING REFRAIN, IS LIKE A MORNING SORROW SONG...
With the end of Reconstruction, and a series of agricultural depressions, life for blacks in the South became increasingly miserable. Lynchings peaked at over 100 per year during the 1890s.
During that decade, white Democrats enforced new Black Codes, the "Jim Crow Laws," segregating transit, schools, and public accommodations. In *Plessy v. Ferguson* in 1896, the Supreme Court upheld such "separate but equal" treatment 7-1.
FEELING SEPARATE, HARLAN?
AND THE EQUAL OF ALL OF YOU PUT TOGETHER.
By 1902, Democrats had replaced the last of the Reconstruction-era state constitutions in the South. The new constitutions disenfranchised blacks with poll taxes, literacy tests, and complex procedures. Whites could apply "grandfather clauses" to escape such requirements.
VOTE HERE
IF YOU CAN READ OR EXPLAIN THE PLAIN MEANING OF THIS CONSTITUTION, THEN YOU CAN VOTE.
THE PLAIN MEANING OF THIS CONSTITUTION IS THAT I *CAN'T* VOTE.
In 1915, as if blacks didn't have enough problems, the Ku Klux Klan returned.
BIRTH OF A NATION
I DON'T THINK THEY GOT GENERAL GRANT BACK FOR THE SEQUEL, EITHER.

But what to do? In his "Atlanta Address," delivered in 1895 to a primarily white audience, the educator Booker T. Washington called for black economic self-sufficiency, practical education, and voluntary self-segregation. Improve black peoples' lives, he preached, and leave the laws until a more propitious time.

In 1909, the sociologist W.E.B. DuBois founded, with white allies, the National Association for the Advancement of Colored People. He rejected Washington's broad-based, incrementalist position in favor of constant agitation and the education of an elite black "Talented Tenth" to carry on the political struggle.

In practical fact, neither program could be carried out in the Jim Crow South. Beginning in 1915, the black-published *Chicago Defender* newspaper began propagandizing for a "Great Migration." With the supply of immigrants cut back by WWI, Northern cities needed labor more than they needed to stay lily-white.

Life in the North, restricted to ghettos and low-wage jobs, was still harsh. But it was enough of an improvement that half a million Southern blacks came north between 1915 and 1920, and twice that in the next decade.

Teddy Roosevelt had promised to serve only two terms.
I DID?
So he picked his secretary of War, William Howard Taft, as his successor in 1908. Taft easily beat three-time loser William Jennings Bryan.
TAFT IS A GENUINE PROGRESSIVE!
Roosevelt and Taft were both Progressive Republicans, but there were Progressives in both parties, with much the same agenda.
MUNICIPAL CONTROL OF UTILITIES. PROFESSIONAL ADMINISTRATION. NO SPOILS SYSTEM. GRADUATED INCOME TAX. BREAKUP OF MONOPOLIES. REGULATION OF CORPORATIONS. CHILD LABOR LAWS. SLUM CLEARANCE. MINIMUM WAGE LAWS. LAND CONSERVATION.
In the spirit of the age, Progressives wanted to direct society efficiently and scientifically. John Dewey reinvented American education theory.
2X2=4
3X2=6
4X2=8
5X2=10
NEW SCHOOLS FOR OLD...
MCGUFFEY'S READER
Frederick Winslow Taylor reinvented the factory floor, introducing "scientific management."
Some Progressives even tried to scientifically manage the species, calling for eugenics to cull the "unfit." Between 1907 and 1963, over 60,000 Americans were forcibly sterilized under state eugenics laws.
IT IS BETTER FOR ALL THE WORLD, IF INSTEAD OF WAITING TO EXECUTE DEGENERATE OFFSPRING FOR CRIME, OR TO LET THEM STARVE FOR THEIR IMBECILITY, SOCIETY CAN PREVENT THOSE WHO ARE MANIFESTLY UNFIT FROM CONTINUING THEIR KIND ... THREE GENERATIONS OF IMBECILES ARE ENOUGH.

In some ways, Taft was at least twice the Progressive that Roosevelt was. In one term, he set aside as much federal land for conservation as Roosevelt had in two.
He launched 80 anti-trust lawsuits to Roosevelt's 44, including the one that broke up Standard Oil in 1911.
DON'T WORRY ABOUT ME! I DOUBLED MY MONEY IN THE NEXT TWO YEARS!
But Roosevelt ran against Taft in the 1912 Republican primaries, which he won …
GET OUT OF MY SPOTLIGHT!
… but party bosses gave Taft the nomination. Roosevelt ran as a Progressive third-party candidate, splitting the GOP enough to elect the Virginia Democrat, Woodrow Wilson, with 42% of the vote.
TSK TSK. WE'RE ALL PROGRESSIVES HERE.
Wilson immediately re-segregated the federal government.
SEGREGATION IS NOT HUMILIATING, BUT A BENEFIT, AND OUGHT TO BE SO REGARDED BY YOU GENTLEMEN.

America's fiscal situation was potentially straightened out with the ratification of the Sixteenth Amendment, allowing an income tax ...
ONE PERCENT?!? IT'S AN OUTRAGE.
TAKE HEART, SIR. MINE IS SEVEN PERCENT.
YOU SURE YOU'RE A DEMOCRAT? YOU LOOK KINDA BRITISH TO ME.
... and the passage of the Federal Reserve Act, creating (for the third time) a central bank of the United States.
Mexico, meanwhile, was fighting a civil war. In 1914, Wilson ordered the U.S. Navy to occupy Veracruz to enforce his arms embargo against one side.
The Mexican warlord Pancho Villa resented Wilson taking sides, especially since Wilson didn't take his side. So he raided Columbus, New Mexico, in 1916, and ran back into Old Mexico ahead of a U.S. Army invasion.
WHEN WERE THESE MAPS LAST UPDATED, 1847?
Europe was in an even bigger mess: World War I broke out in 1914. The British blockaded German trade and borrowed American money to buy American weapons.
NOW, REMEMBER, WE'RE NEUTRAL.
WE'D HAPPILY DO BUSINESS WITH GERMANY, TOO, BUT THEY CAN'T GET ANY MONEY TO US ...
... AND WE CAN'T GET ANY WEAPONS TO THEM.
Germany turned to submarine warfare to break the blockade, sinking the British passenger liner RMS Lusitania – and killing 128 Americans – on May 7, 1915.
WHY WOULD THE BARBAROUS HUN ATTACK US?
I'M SURE IT HAD NOTHING TO DO WITH THE 4,000 ARTILLERY SHELLS AND 4.2 MILLION RIFLE BULLETS IN THE HOLD.

Wilson protested vigorously, refused to increase military spending, and then ran for re-election in 1916, winning a knife-edge victory.
HE KEPT US OUT OF WAR
KEPT
NOTE THE PAST TENSE.
A month after his inauguration, responding to renewed German submarine attacks, Wilson asked Congress to declare war on Germany and its allies.
Wilson set up the Office of Public Information to distribute wartime propaganda. Its 75,000 volunteers tapped phones, opened mail, and spied on their neighbors.
BACK THE HUN
QUIE
HEY, ANYTHING TO HELP MAKE THE WORLD SAFE FOR DEMOCRACY.
WANT YOU
In May 1917, Congress passed the Selective Service Act. America had a draft again.
The Espionage and Sedition Acts made it illegal to criticize the government or the war effort, or to protest the draft. In 1918, Eugene V. Debs was convicted of violating them.
BACK AGAIN SO SOON, MR. DEBS?
I THINK THIS SEDITION ACT IS UNCONSTITUTIONAL.
YEAH, MR. JEFFERSON SAID THE SAME THING.
Leaving Bizbee, Arizona
In the climate of hysteria, German newspapers were shut down, hamburgers became "Liberty Sandwiches," and socialists, Mexicans, and anybody else suspicious were run out of town on a rail … sometimes, literally.

World War I was unimaginable hell to Americans. It had introduced poison gas, tanks, flame-throwers, and aerial bombardment to warfare. Trenches stretched 400 miles across Europe.
The first three years of the war – and incompetent Allied strategy – had killed 540,000 British and Commonwealth soldiers, 640,000 Italians, and over a million Frenchmen.
OVER THE TOP
By comparison, in 1917 the entire U.S. Army was 120,000 regulars, with 900 artillery pieces. Nevertheless, America's war would still have to be a ground game.
OVER THERE! OVER THERE! WE'D BETTER GET SOME MORE MEN OR IT'S OVER, OVER THERE!
At the beginning of the war, the U.S. Army Air Service had no combat aircraft. At the end of the war, there were only 196 American built planes in combat, despite spending $840 million.
$4,285,714.30 EACH
Wilson appointed "Black Jack" Pershing to command the American Expeditionary Force, which he immediately started building from scratch in France.
JUST GIVE US WARM AMERICAN BODIES FOR OUR ARMIES, THERE'S A GOOD CHAP.
EH, I THINK I'LL KEEP THE YANKS UNDER MY COMMAND. WHAT HAPPENED TO ALL THE MEN YOU HAD, ANYHOW?
WE, ER, KILLED THEM ALL.
WELL, NOW I'M SURE I'LL KEEP THE YANKS UNDER MY COMMAND.

Just as the Americans were entering the war, the Russians were leaving it. In October 1917, the Communists overthrew Russia's democratic government and sued for peace with Germany.
NO MAS! NO MAS!
The Germans shifted 500,000 men from the East and smashed into France in a desperate gamble to win the war.
VE MUST BEAT THE AMERIKANERS TO PARIS!
JA, OR ZEY VILL TAKE ALL ZE GOOD PARKING SPOTS!
At Belleau Wood in June 1918, the U.S. Marine Corps stopped them – at the cost of 55% casualties. It was the first successful Allied infantry assault against entrenched German troops in the entire war.
THE GERMANS ARE COMING! RETREAT!
RETREAT? HELL, WE JUST GOT HERE!
On September 12-15, the AEF – using tanks in combat for the first time in American history – pushed the Germans back 15 miles, retaking St.-Mihiel. Commanding the tanks was Lt. Col. George S. Patton.
I COULD GET USED TO THIS.
Over the next two months, 2 million strong, the AEF chewed up German forces in the Argonne Forest. Defeated in France, the Germans requested an armistice. On November 11, 1918, World War I ended. 116,708 American soldiers were dead.

By 1919, things on the home front were worse than on the Western Front. Wartime inflation was 100%, income taxes had rocketed up to 77%, and government bureaucrats still imposed wartime controls on food, phones, fuel, and railroads despite the armistice.
HE KEPT US OUT OF BREAD, MORE LIKE.
New England telephone operators and textile workers, New York printers and teamsters, San Francisco and New Orleans stevedores, Boston police, Pittsburgh steelworkers, L.A. streetcar drivers, even Hollywood actors – 20% of the national workforce – went on strike in 1919. The entire city of Seattle went on strike for a week in February.
THE NUMBER YOU HAVE REACHED IS AN EXPLOITIVE CRIMINAL THAT DRAINS THE BLOOD OF THE WORKING CLASS.
A series of terrorist bombings struck the U.S. Mail and targets in eight cities, including the home of Attorney General Mitchell Palmer.
I REALLY LIKED THAT HOUSE.
Unemployment hit 12%, and 25 cities erupted in race riots that summer as jobless whites fought back against the Great Migration; in Chicago, 23 blacks and 15 whites died.
I KILLED PLENTY OF KRAUTS, I CAN SURELY KILL A KLANSMAN.
America was also undergoing the worst epidemic in its history, the "Spanish flu," which began at Ft. Riley, Kansas, in 1918 and eventually killed 600,000 Americans – the same death toll as the Civil War – by 1920.
I HAD A LITTLE BIRD ITS NAME WAS ENZA I OPENED UP THE WINDOW AND IN FLEW ENZA.
QUARANTINE
Some American troops remained overseas, invading Siberia to assist anti-Communist "White" forces until 1920, and occupying part of Germany until the final peace in 1923.
WHY ARE WE HERE, AGAIN, SARGE?
WE'RE HERE TO KEEP RUSSIA WHITE.
WELL, MISSION ACCOMPLISHED.

Wilson initially proposed "Fourteen Points" as the basis of a peace settlement in January of 1918. The Allies reacted with scorn: Clemenceau of France noted that "God only needed Ten."

I. No secret diplomacy

II. Freedom of the seas

III. Free trade

IV. Arms reductions

V. A voice for the colonies

VI. Evacuation of Russia

VII. Restore Belgium

VIII. Alsace-Lorraine to France

IX. Tyrol and Fiume to Italy

X. Democracy in Austria-Hungary

XI. Balkan readjustments

XII. Autonomy in Turkey

XIII. Independent Poland

XIV. League of Nations

By October, Wilson had secretly agreed to strip Germany of its colonies, dismember Austria-Hungary, accede to current British sea law, and demand reparations from Germany.

At the 1919 peace conference at Versailles, Wilson bargained away six more of the Points so the Allies would accede to his League of Nations.

After a terrific fight, during which Wilson suffered a debilitating stroke, Congress rejected the Versailles Treaty.

Wilson remained an invalid for the remainder of his term, his wife, Edith, essentially running the government over his forged signature.

Attorney General Palmer reacted to the chaos of 1919 by launching a series of raids; arresting 10,000 suspected anarchists, socialists, and other radicals; and eventually deporting 550 aliens without trial.

Worst of all, you couldn't even drink to forget. Prohibition became the law of the land with ratification of the Eighteenth Amendment in 1920.

Perhaps unsurprisingly, the Republican Warren G. Harding won in the biggest landslide in American history.
LET US HAVE A RETURN TO NORMALCY.

Eugene V. Debs had run for President from prison on the Socialist ticket and got 900,000 votes; Harding commuted his sentence, and freed the other radicals imprisoned by Wilson for sedition.
GIVE MY BEST TO PRESIDENT HARDING, MR. DEBS.
JAIL

Harding also created the Veterans' Bureau and the Office of the Budget, and appointed William Howard Taft as Chief Justice of the Supreme Court.

But nonetheless Harding's reputation suffered; he was a favorite target of America's two top humorists. Will Rogers, despite meeting Harding, apparently didn't like him.
MY VIEWS ON EUROPEAN AFFAIRS ARE SO IN ACCORD WITH YOU, MR. PRESIDENT, THAT I MIGHT ALMOST BE SUSPECTED OF BEING A DEMOCRAT.

And the journalist and wordsmith H.L. Mencken took Harding's prose style personally.
HE WRITES THE WORST ENGLISH THAT I HAVE EVER ENCOUNTERED.
IT REMINDS ME OF A STRING OF WET SPONGES; IT REMINDS ME OF TATTERED WASHING ON THE LINE; IT REMINDS ME OF STALE BEAN SOUP, OF COLLEGE YELLS, OF DOGS BARKING IDIOTICALLY THROUGH ENDLESS NIGHTS. IT IS SO BAD THAT A SORT OF GRANDEUR CREEPS INTO IT.

It didn't help that Harding presided over the most corrupt administration since Grant's. His Interior secretary took bribes to lease public oilfields, the director of the Veterans' Bureau sold medicine on the black market, the head of the Alien Property Office embezzled alien property, and his attorney general was almost impeached for bootlegging.
ALMOST IMPEACHED! DOESN'T COUNT!

The stress of those scandals destroyed Harding's health and he died of pneumonia in 1923, making Vice President Calvin Coolidge the President.
...
Coolidge was elected in his own right the next year, not least because the economy was booming. Real per capita income increased by almost 40% in the 1920s, helped along by generous tax cuts in all brackets.
Education spending nearly doubled, too, setting the stage for a new conflict between Progressive educators and fundamentalist Christians. In 1925, William Jennings Bryan successfully prosecuted John D. Scopes for teaching human evolution in Tennessee.
SCIENCE IS A MAGNIFICENT FORCE, BUT IT IS NOT A TEACHER OF MORALS. IT CAN PERFECT MACHINERY, BUT IT ADDS NO MORAL RESTRAINTS TO PROTECT SOCIETY FROM THE MISUSE OF THE MACHINE.
Thanks in large part to Mencken, who dubbed it the "Monkey Trial," this tactical victory became a cultural defeat, and fundamentalism retreated from the political scene for 50 years.
WHAT DO YOU THINK?
I DO NOT THINK ABOUT THINGS I DON'T THINK ABOUT.
WELL, SOMETIMES.
DO YOU THINK ABOUT THINGS YOU DO THINK ABOUT?
In 1924, however, Congress decided there wasn't enough prosperity to go around, and sharply restricted immigration, especially from southern and eastern Europe. Immigration from China and Japan was banned entirely.
CLOSED. THIS MEANS YOU!

If fewer Europeans came to America, more Americans were going to Europe. The most famous of them, Charles Lindbergh, went alone in 1927.
A whole "Lost Generation" of them went to Paris, where even a struggling writer could live well thanks to the strong dollar.
BULLFIGHTING IS ...
... WE SEEK THE GREAT FORGOTTEN LANGUAGE ...
ITS ONE WILL -- FLOW!
... ON SIFTINGS IN OBLIVION.
... IS A ROSE IS A ROSE.
SHE WAS A FADED BUT STILL LOVELY ...
IF THERE IS A SPECIAL HELL FOR WRITERS ...
The poet T.S. Eliot went to England.

Back in America, words jumped off the page in 1927 as sound came to the movies.
WAIT A MINUTE, WAIT A MINUTE, YOU AIN'T HEARD NOTHIN' YET!

It was the Jazz Age; Louis Armstrong formed his Hot Five in Chicago in 1925.

American classical music took off, too. George Gershwin composed "Rhapsody in Blue" in 1924.
"My people are American, my time is today ... music must repeat the thought and aspirations of the times."

The same year, Aaron Copland composed his first symphony.
"I don't compose. I assemble materials."

Americans listened to this new music – and much more – on their new radios. In 1921, a manager at the brand-new Radio Corporation of America, David Sarnoff, arranged the broadcast of the Jack Dempsey title fight over the radio in order to sell more sets. 300,000 Americans were instantly hooked.
DEMPSEY SMASHES CARPENTIER -- IT'S A KNOCKOUT! JACK DEMPSEY HAS WON THE FIRST MILLION-DOLLAR PURSE IN BOXING!

By 1928, under Sarnoff's impetus RCA had spun off a radio network, the National Broadcasting Company, with a national audience of 35 million.
RCA
NBC

More ominously, RCA stock went from 85½ to 420 in 1928, and hit 549 the next year, when it was the most-traded stock on Wall Street despite a ludicrous price-to-earnings ratio of 73. A stock bubble was blowing up.
GIMME SOME O' THAT INTERNATIONAL COMBUSTION ENGINEERING! I HEAR IT'S THE BEE'S KNEES!
THAT'S $ 102 PER SHARE.
I DON'T HAVE THAT MUCH ON ME ... I'LL TAKE A HUNNERT SHARES AN' OWE YOU!
Coolidge declined to run in 1928; his technocratic secretary of Commerce, Herbert Hoover, replaced him on the Republican ticket, and won handily.
PRESIDENT COOLIDGE, WHAT ABOUT THE LONG-TERM ECONOMIC SITUATION?
WE'LL LEAVE THAT TO THE WONDER BOY.
And then came the Crash. In the week between "Black Thursday" on October 24 and "Black Tuesday" on October 29, the stock market shed $30 billion, or about the cost of World War I. By 1933, those losses would be tripled.

Next, banks started failing at increasing rates: 1,350 in 1930 alone, with $140 billion in deposits vanishing by 1933. By 1939, 9,000 banks would fail. Credit went from too easy to "too bad." Industrial production dropped by half.
Brother, can you spare $286 MILLION?

Hoover tried everything to fix what had become the Great Depression. He tried tax cuts and tax increases. He tried massive public works spending.
HOOVER DAM PROJECT
GOLDEN GATE BRIDGE PROJECT
CALIFORNIA AQUEDUCT

Congress helped, too, by passing the gigantic Smoot-Hawley tariff of 1930, which destroyed international trade and helped crash banks in Britain and Germany.

Meanwhile, Hoover tried making inspiring speeches, which inspired nobody.
IF THERE SHALL BE NO RETREAT, IF THE ATTACK SHALL CONTINUE AS IT IS NOW ORGANIZED, THEN THIS BATTLE IS WON.
HELLO? IS THIS THING ON?
BLAH

He convinced business to keep wages high, which naturally sent unemployment through the roof: 24.9% by the end of his term.
WHAT A TERRIFIC HEADLINE FOR US, MR. PRESIDENT! YOU'VE JUST SIGNED AMERICA'S FIRST UNEMPLOYMENT ASSISTANCE PROGRAM!
MAKE SURE YOU PICK UP AN APPLICATION FOR IT ON YOUR WAY OUT THE DOOR.

In 1932, 17,000 unemployed WWI veterans camped out in Washington to pressure Congress to pass a bill paying their promised bonus early. When D.C. police could not clear out the "Bonus Army," Hoover sent in the troops.
THE SECRETARY OF WAR SAYS WE'RE BEING TREATED WITH "UNPARALLELED KINDNESS."
I SUPPOSE THAT'S TECHNICALLY TRUE.

Hoover, of course, was crushed in the 1932 election by the Democrat Franklin D. Roosevelt, a cousin of Theodore Roosevelt. The national mood immediately brightened …
LET ME ASSERT MY BELIEF THAT THE ONLY THING WE HAVE TO FEAR IS FEAR ITSELF.
… because Prohibition was on its way to repeal, via the Twenty-first Amendment.
Twenty-first Amendment to the U.S. Constitution
Section 1: What Were We Thinking?
Section 2: No, Seriously.
Since Prohibition had been such a success, Harry Anslinger, head of the Federal Bureau of Narcotics, began pressing for a national prohibition of marijuana, which passed in 1937. America had its first "war on drugs."
But FDR had bigger fish to fry. In his first 100 days in office, Roosevelt pushed bill after bill through a special session of Congress. His "New Deal" was much more Hooverism with much better style.
THE BANKS HAVE SHUT DOWN IN 32 STATES!
THERE'S GOING TO BE A RUN ON GOLD WHEN PEOPLE FIGURE THAT OUT!
YOU'RE JUST MAKING THIS UP AS YOU GO ALONG, AREN'T YOU, SIR?
THEN SHUT THEM DOWN IN ALL 48 AND CALL IT A "BANK HOLIDAY."
THEN WE'LL GO OFF THE GOLD STANDARD AND MAKE OWNING GOLD ILLEGAL.
He used the Dust Bowl – a severe Western drought caused by a strong La Niña effect in the Pacific from 1930 to 1938 – to help justify farm subsidies and the CCC work relief program.
I'M FROM THE GOVERNMENT-- THE PRESIDENT IS GOING TO PAY YOU NOT TO PLANT THIS YEAR.
THAT WON'T BE A CONCERN.
Roosevelt took "gas-and-water socialism" to its heights with the Tennessee Valley Authority, a network of dams and drainage projects that provided an impoverished region with subsidized electricity and flood control – at the cost of relocating 15,000 people.
DAM!

In 1935, Congress passed the Wagner Act, guaranteeing the right to organize unions, strike, and bargain collectively. FDR stayed out of a string of strikes that resulted in John L. Lewis' brand-new, harder-line Congress of Industrial Organizations growing to 2.7 million workers by 1941.
I HAVE PLEADED LABOR'S CASE, NOT IN THE QUAVERING TONES OF A FEEBLE MENDICANT ASKING ALMS, BUT IN THE THUNDERING VOICE OF THE CAPTAIN OF A MIGHTY HOST, DEMANDING THE RIGHTS TO WHICH FREE MEN ARE ENTITLED."
In 1936, Roosevelt and the Democrats won a crushing re-election victory and increased their Congressional majorities.
THAT'S 2.7 MILLION MORE WORKERS WHO'LL VOTE DEMOCRATIC NOW ... HOW MANY OLD FOLKS WOULD YOU SAY THERE ARE, HARRY?
ABOUT 3.5 MILLION?
I FEEL A SOCIAL SECURITY PLAN COMING ON ...
With his new mandate, in 1937 FDR decided to curb the Supreme Court, which had ruled many of his New Deal programs unconstitutional.
IF YOU DON'T START LETTING THE NEW DEAL THROUGH, I'M GOING TO ADD SIX MORE JUSTICES.
HOW DARE YOU TRY TO BULLY THIS COURT! WE WON'T STAND FOR IT! AND ON AN ENTIRELY UNRELATED SUBJECT, YOU'LL BE PLEASED TO KNOW THAT THE COURT FINDS THE WAGNER ACT CONSTITUTIONAL.
But such overreaching, all those CIO strikes, and the fact that the Depression continued without much letup – unemployment in 1938 was 19% – let the Republicans come back in Congress in 1938. Allied with conservative Democrats, they could block any more Roosevelt radicalism. The New Deal was over.
X
F
D
I
C
W
P
A
S
E
C
Not everyone was depressed. The Roosevelt era was also the Golden Age of Hollywood.
SHOWING
NOW SHOWING
KING KONG
CITIZEN KAN
In 1938, kids got happier, too, as the Golden Age of Comic Books began.
ACTION COMICS

Adolf Hitler's expansionist Nazi Germany began making noise during Roosevelt's second term.
I ALSO HAFF EIN NEW DEAL FOR FULL EMPLOYMENT UND MASSIVE GOVERNMENT ACTION.
Isolationists in Congress passed the Neutrality Act of 1935 to keep the noise down, and kept amending it as the noise level increased.
NEITHER THE U.S. GOVERNMENT NOR U.S. FIRMS MAY SUPPLY WEAPONS TO ANY BELLIGERENT POWER, OR TRAVEL ON THEIR SHIPS.
OR LOAN THEM MONEY, OR PROVIDE CREDITS.
THIS COUNTS FOR CIVIL WARS, TOO. AND STRATEGIC MINERALS.
Despite Republican mutterings, Roosevelt won an unprecedented third term in 1940, mostly because World War II had started in 1939. Hitler's Germany had smashed France and menaced Britain.
I HAVE SAID THIS BEFORE, BUT I SHALL SAY IT AGAIN AND AGAIN AND AGAIN. YOUR BOYS ARE NOT GOING TO BE SENT TO ANY FOREIGN WAR.
WHICH MEANS WE'LL BE AT WAR BY NEXT YEAR, THEN.
In 1941, Roosevelt rammed through the "Lend-Lease" program …
I NOTICE IT DOESN'T SAY ANYTHING HERE ABOUT JUST GIVING WAR MATERIEL TO BRITAIN. I'LL DO THAT, THEN.
… and ordered the U.S. Navy to convoy American supplies to Britain.
Japan, meanwhile, had invaded China. In response, the United States embargoed steel, scrap metal, and eventually oil shipments to Japan.
Opposing Roosevelt's "march to war," Charles Lindbergh led a growing peace movement.

The Japanese attack on the U.S. Naval base at Pearl Harbor, Hawaii, sank five ships, killed 2,402 Americans, and made Lindbergh and the isolationists irrelevant. An overconfident Hitler, allied with Japan in the Axis, declared war on the United States on December 11. The United States was at war again.

The Japanese onslaught took the Philippines, Guam, and Wake Island, and had reached the Aleutians at the tip of Alaska by June of 1942.
ALEUTIAN ISLANDS
GUAM
WAKE ISLAND
PEARL HARBOR
HAWAIIAN ISLANDS
PHILLIPPINES
The Japanese treated American P.O.W.s with utter brutality, beginning with the "Bataan Death March," a five-day ordeal during which 650 American and perhaps 10,000 Filipinos died.
President Roosevelt and California governor Earl Warren reacted by interning 48,000 Japanese aliens – and 72,000 American citizens of Japanese descent – in remote "internment camps."
YOU'RE RELOCATING THE GERMANS TOO, RIGHT?
WELL, WE'RE MOVING ADMIRAL NIMITZ AND GENERAL EISENHOWER OUT OF CALIFORNIA, IF THAT'S WHAT YOU'RE ASKING.
Racial tensions were not restricted to Japanese-Americans. The Great Migration accelerated as war industries hired more blacks; in 1943, a race riot in Detroit killed 25 blacks and 9 whites. The "zoot suit riot" in Los Angeles that year pitted sailors against Mexican-Americans.
WHY YOU BASHING ON ME, MAN?
YOU'RE DRESSED FUNNY!
YOU'RE ONE TO TALK!
American experts broke the Japanese naval code, allowing Admiral Chester Nimitz to stop the Japanese in the Battle of the Coral Sea and maul their fleet at Midway in June 1942. By August, the United States had counter-attacked, landing on Guadalcanal Island.

U.S. Army Chief of Staff George C. Marshall helped plan the "Europe First" strategy – America would defeat Germany before crushing Japan. With the U.S. Army unready for major combat, "Europe First" began with a bombing campaign.
GET USED TO IT, FRITZ! THERE'S 95,000 MORE WHERE THIS ONE CAME FROM!
Those bombers, and much more, came from American factories, "the Arsenal of Democracy." By December 1942, the United States was out-producing the entire Axis put together. The Great Depression ended with full employment – and with 6 million women working in factories for the first time.
Construction magnate Henry J. Kaiser used women welders to build his "Liberty Ships," which carried Lend-Lease to Soviet Russia and Britain.
KAPITAN, THEY SAY THE AMERIKANERS ARE PRODUCING ONE SHIP EVERY TEN HOURS.
WE'LL BE GETTING LESS SLEEP, THEN.
Long-range bombers, better radar, and sheer numbers finally turned the tide of the Battle of the Atlantic in May 1943. The "wolf packs" were broken.
SAY GOODNIGHT, FRITZ!
In November 1942, American forces landed in North Africa, only to be mauled by the German General Erwin Rommel at Kasserine Pass in February.
Although the United States and Britain pushed the Germans out of Africa, liberated Sicily, and invaded Italy, skillful German defense stalled the Allied advance by October 1943.
AT THIS RATE, WE'LL BE IN BERLIN BY CHRISTMAS.
CHRISTMAS?
BERLIN 1,065 MILES
OF 1959.

Soviet dictator Joseph Stalin demanded a real "Second Front." His Red Army was doing almost all the work of the war. The Soviets lost over 14 million soldiers in WWII, and caused 80% of all German casualties. Without U.S. Lend-Lease shipments – especially trucks, boots, and locomotives – the Red Army would grind to a halt, but production wasn't the same as fighting.
HEY, IVAN, IT SAYS HERE THAT THE AMERICANS HAVE LANDED IN MOROCCO.
On June 6, 1944, D-Day, America entered the war for real. Despite suffering over 6,500 casualties on the first day, the U.S. Army broke through the German defenses in Normandy and landed 314,000 men in France over the next two weeks.
YOU ARE ABOUT TO EMBARK UPON THE GREAT CRUSADE, TOWARD WHICH WE HAVE STRIVEN THESE MANY MONTHS. THE EYES OF THE WORLD ARE UPON YOU. THE HOPE AND PRAYERS OF LIBERTY-LOVING PEOPLE EVERYWHERE MARCH WITH YOU.
General Patton thrust across France, successfully capturing 50,000 German troops and 10,000 vehicles with his American blitzkrieg.
!?
NEXT GAS TWO MONTHS
In the Pacific, General Douglas MacArthur landed at Leyte in the Philippines in October 1944. The Battle of Leyte Gulf the next month essentially destroyed the Japanese navy.
I HAVE RETURNED.
A December German counter-attack through the Ardennes Forest left a dangerous "bulge" in Allied lines. American troops held out inside the bulge until Patton's forces relieved them.

With the German Army wrecked in the Bulge, the door was open for the Allies. As U.S. troops rolled through Germany, they liberated concentration camps where the Nazis had enslaved Jews and other "undesirables." Invading from the east, the Russians discovered something worse yet: extermination camps.

With victory in sight, Stalin, Roosevelt (now in his fourth term), and Churchill met at Yalta in February 1945 to plan the postwar world.

The "island-hopping" campaign continued in the Pacific. Iwo Jima fell in March 1945.

Okinawa took three months to fall, during which time its 90,000 Japanese defenders killed 12,500 Americans and 140,000 Okinawans. Next stop: Japan itself.

In April, Roosevelt died. Vice President Harry S Truman became president, and discovered that FDR hadn't told him everything.

Inspired by a letter from Albert Einstein, FDR had ordered a crash program to invent, and then build, an atomic bomb. It was very close to completion when Germany surrendered on May 7, 1945.

"The enemy now possesses a new and terrible weapon with the power to destroy many innocent lives and do incalculable damage. Should we continue to fight, not only would it result in an ultimate collapse and obliteration of the Japanese nation, but also it would lead to the total extinction of human civilization.
– Emperor Hirohito of Japan, August 14, 1945
By Truman's order, the United States dropped the first atomic bomb on Hiroshima, Japan, on August 6, 1945. America dropped the second atomic bomb on Nagasaki, Japan, on August 9, 1945. Japan surrendered five days later. Two bombs had killed 140,000 people. World War II was over, and something else had begun.

PART FIVE

TEAR DOWN THIS WALL *1945-NOW*

"General Secretary Gorbachev, if you seek peace, if you seek prosperity for the Soviet Union and Eastern Europe, if you seek liberalization: Come here to this gate! Mr. Gorbachev, open this gate! Mr. Gorbachev, tear down this wall!"
– Ronald Reagan, at the Berlin Wall, June 12, 1987

The war was over, and the armed forces dropped from 12 million men to 1.5 million in two years.
BABY, LET'S GET MARRIED AND HAVE 76 MILLION KIDS WHO WILL GROW UP TO REJECT EVERYTHING WE STAND FOR.
Congress passed the "GI Bill" in 1944, which subsidized veterans' education and housing after the war.
ALL THOSE OPPOSED TO HAVING TO DEAL WITH ANOTHER "BONUS ARMY" AFTER THIS WAR, SAY 'AYE'.
AYE!
But more than 10 million new workers – and consumers – still jolted the economy into inflation and unemployment.
IT MAY COMFORT YOU TO KNOW THAT THINGS WERE TWICE AS BAD IN 1919.
NEW 1946 MODEL!
OUT OF GERMANY AND OUT OF WORK
TO ERR IS TRUMAN
In 1946, the wartime "no strikes" agreement broke down, and 10% of the U.S. work force, including the entire cities of Rochester, Houston, and Oakland, went out. Truman responded by nationalizing key industries for the duration of the strikes.
THE STEEL STOPS HERE
THE PHONES STOP HERE
THE ELECTRICITY STOPS HERE
THE BUCK STOPS HERE
THE COAL STOPS HERE
THE TRAINS STOP HERE
THE MEAT PACKING STOPS HERE
THE SHIPS STOP HERE
Congress responded with the Taft-Hartley Act, passed over Truman's veto in 1947. Union membership began declining from its postwar peak of 36% of the work force.
READ 'EM AND WEEP: WE GOT A "MANDATORY COOLING DOWN PERIOD," SYMPATHY STRIKES AND CLOSED SHOPS ARE OUTLAWED, RIGHT-TO-WORK IS LEGAL, AND THE WAGNER ACT NOW COVERS UNION TACTICS, TOO.
I WANT A NEW DEAL.
YOU ALREADY HAD ONE OF THOSE.

The mass mobilizations of unionism and wartime during the 1930s and 1940s also spilled into America's arts. "Big-band" swing dominated jazz, and big-studio animation drove comics.
The Edison-style "lone inventor" was replaced by the Edison-style corporate research laboratory. Charles Carlson invented xerography in his garage in 1938; only when Haloid (later Xerox) bought, refined, and marketed it in 1948 did it succeed.
Corporate research labs brought forth the microwave oven (from Raytheon in 1945); the improved magnetic tape (from Ampex in 1946); and, most important of all, the transistor (from Bell Labs in 1947).
The mass man wanted mass consumption …
… and paid for it with the credit card (from Diners Club in 1950).
the Diners' Club

At the Potsdam Conference in June 1945, two models of the mass man collided.
PRESIDENT ROOSEVELT DIED, AND I BECAME PRESIDENT.
I BECAME GENERAL SECRETARY, AND KILLED 20 MILLION PEOPLE.

Stalin, at least, proved more interested in mass consumption of Europe than of refrigerators.
WE ALREADY HAVE SIBERIA TO KEEP THINGS COLD!
ROPE

The Soviets were stirring things up in Greece, Turkey, Iran, Finland, Japan, and even the newly founded UN.
UN CELEBRATING NEARLY ONE YEAR OF WORLD PEACE
CAPITALIST, MONARCHIST, ROADER! FASCIST LAP DOG!
BLOODY-MINDED SUBVERSIVE! COMMUNIST TYRANT!
WELL, THAT DIDN'T LAST LONG.

Truman wanted it stopped. He invited Churchill to America ...
FROM STETTIN IN THE BALTIC TO TRIESTE IN THE ADRIATIC AN IRON CURTAIN HAS DESCENDED ACROSS THE CONTINENT.

... and invited America back into Europe with the 1947 "Truman Doctrine."
IT IS THE POLICY OF THE UNITED STATES TO SUPPORT FREE PEOPLES WHO ARE RESISTING ATTEMPTED SUBJUGATION BY ARMED MINORITIES OR BY OUTSIDE PRESSURES
WHAT ABOUT SUPPORTING DICTATORSHIPS?
I'LL HAVE TO GET BACK TO YOU ON THAT.

Truman then offered "Marshall Plan" aid – eventually $13 billion worth – to war-ravaged Europe, including the Soviets and their satellites.
WHO WANTS FREE MONEY?
NO! IT'S A TRICK! THERE ARE STRINGS ATTACHED!
EUROPE

Recipient nations broadly liberalized trade and money policy, joining the United States in the "Bretton Woods system." The General Agreement on Tariffs and Trade (GATT) spurred a global recovery and a 30-year boom in Europe.
WELL, IT WOULD REALLY HELP EVERYONE OUT IF Y'ALL WOULD GET RICH ENOUGH TO BUY OUR GOODS AGAIN.
SEE! I TOLD YOU IT WAS A TRICK!
EUR

Competition with the Communists focused new attention on the less free parts of America.
LOOK HOW AMERICA DISCRIMINATES AGAINST ITS MINORITIES! IN THE SOVIET UNION, WE KILL ALL PEOPLE EQUALLY. ESPECIALLY MINORITIES.
In 1948, Truman desegregated the U.S. military by executive order.
THE SEGREGATION STOPS HERE
A year earlier, Jackie Robinson desegregated baseball by sheer guts.
In 1948, the unpopular Truman managed to split the Democratic Party three ways. The Republicans united behind New York governor Thomas Dewey, who said as little as possible.
HE'S TOO MEAN TO THE COMMUNISTS!
HE'S TOO NICE TO THE N****S!
THE FUTURE LIES AHEAD OF US.
Truman went on a national "whistle-stop" campaign, hammering hard at the "Do-Nothing Congress."
GIVE 'EM HELL, HARRY!
I JUST TELL THE TRUTH ABOUT THEM AND THEY THINK IT'S HELL!
Nevertheless, the media thought Truman was dead in the water. Not for the first or last time, they got the story wrong.
DEWEY DEFEATS TRUMAN

But five terms of one-party rule bred corruption. Congress investigated the IRS for fixing taxes; a special prosecutor forced 166 IRS resignations or firings before Truman's attorney general fired him. Truman's military aide peddled favors for businessmen.
PSST! WANT SOME EUROPEAN PERFUME? I CAN GET IT FOR YOU CHEAP.
Congress was even more enthusiastic about investigating Communists in Truman's administration, including Soviet agents Harry Dexter White (head of the IMF), Judith Coplon (of the Justice Department), and Alger Hiss (a former State Department official) ...
... and several hundred less-guilty parties. Wisconsin Senator Joseph McCarthy was particularly eager to launch headline-grabbing "investigations."
I HAVE HERE A LIST! A LIST OF 205 ... ER, 57 ... ER, 115 NAMES OF HIGH GOVERNMENT OFFICIALS ACTIVELY AIDING SOVIET COMMUNISM.
IS YOUR NAME ON THAT LIST, JOE?
And the "Cold War" was heating up. The Soviets blockaded the Western sectors of Berlin in 1948, but backed down after a massive American airlift supplied the city.
THIS CAN'T END WELL.
In 1949, America and Western Europe joined in the North Atlantic Treaty Organization, a defensive alliance against Soviet aggression.
IT MAY BE ENTANGLING, BUT IT FEELS SO RIGHT!
That same year, however, the Soviets detonated their own atomic bomb, and mainland China fell to the Communists.

On June 25, 1950, with Stalin's go-ahead, Communist North Korean dictator Kim Il-Sung invaded South Korea.
38th PARALLEL
Rather than ask Congress for a declaration of war, Truman went to the UN. The United States took advantage of a Soviet walk-out, and the UN approved intervention.
WHAT? WHAT DID I MISS?
Truman put General MacArthur, currently heading the occupation of Japan, in charge of the UN-U.S. forces. MacArthur used war spending as a "Marshall Plan" for Japanese recovery.
GIVE ME $ 3.5 BILLION WORTH OF WAR MATERIEL -- STAT!
MacArthur successfully pulled off a surprise amphibious landing at Inchon, far behind North Korean lines. Cut off, the North Koreans retreated and MacArthur pursued them all the way to the Chinese border.
I HAVE ... ER, ARRIVED!
The Communist Chinese, nervous about a re-unified, pro-American Korea, sent a quarter of a million troops across the border and smashed into the UN forces.
UH, GENERAL?
U.S. and British Marines fought a desperate rear guard action at "Frozen Chosin," mauling six Chinese divisions and buying time for UN evacuation from the North.

As UN forces pushed the Chinese back north again, MacArthur began calling for an escalation of the war into China.
WE ESTIMATE ABOUT 700,000 CHINESE TROOPS IN THE THEATER RIGHT NOW, SIR.
MATT, AS I SEE IT, THE PROBLEM IS WE'RE NOT FIGHTING ENOUGH CHINESE.
GENERAL, WHAT EXACTLY IS IN YOUR PIPE?
Finally, in April 1951, Truman fired MacArthur for insubordination, to howls of media protest.
DAILY TIRADE
IMPEACH DEWEY, ER, TRUMAN
The war settled into a stalemate for two more years, neither side able to gain decisive advantage.
38th PARALLEL
The Republicans nominated Eisenhower for president, who campaigned on a promise to "go to Korea" if elected.
KOREA
Eisenhower won easily, went to Korea, and immediately negotiated an armistice. The United States had suffered over 36,000 battle deaths, but the Korean War was over.
KOREA

During the Korean War, the U.S. Army decided to obey President Truman's 1948 executive order.
I FEAR I MUST REPORT THAT, DUE TO THE RAPIDLY SHIFTING TACTICAL SITUATION DURING THE HIGHEST-STRESS PERIOD OF THE KOREAN CONFLICT, THE UNITED STATES ARMY WAS FORCED, ON AN EMERGENCY BASIS ... TO RACIALLY INTEGRATE ITS UNITS.
In *Brown v. Board of Education* in 1954, the Supreme Court decided to obey the Fourteenth Amendment.
UH, THAT WHOLE *PLESSY V. FERGUSON* THING -- WE WERE JUST KIDDING ABOUT THAT.
President Eisenhower immediately ordered D.C. desegregated, and then the federal government.
IT DIDN'T LOOK ANY BETTER IN THE ORIGINAL GERMAN.
WHITES ONLY
Many Southern whites reacted with violence; the number of lynchings and secret murders climbed again, as in the 1890s. But not all of them could be kept secret: the 1955 murder in Mississippi of Emmett Till, a black teenager from Chicago, became a global scandal.
On December 1, 1955, four days after attending a mass meeting to discuss the Till murder, Montgomery, Alabama seamstress Rosa Parks refused to give her seat on the bus to a white man.
I DON'T THINK I SHOULD HAVE TO STAND UP.
Parks, the NAACP secretary in Montgomery, had intentionally triggered the Montgomery Bus Boycott. For 382 days, despite firebombings and attacks by members of the White Citizens' Council, blacks in Montgomery refused to ride the buses, crippling the bus company. Finally, the Supreme Court ruled that buses could not be segregated. The "Movement" had its first clear victory.
WELL, AT LEAST THEY'S ALL WHITE NOW.
YOU IDJIT.

Bayard Rustin, the architect of that victory, had been arrested and beaten for riding segregated buses as early as 1947, and responded with nonviolence. Rustin studied Thoreau, and observed Thoreau's ideas of civil disobedience in practice in India. He gave the Movement its crucial ideological and tactical underpinnings.

But as a gay man and a former Communist (though he left the Party in disgust in 1941), Rustin could not be the Movement's spokesman. That role went to a blindingly charismatic speaker, Dr. Martin Luther King, Jr., pastor of the Dexter Avenue Baptist Church.

King's right-hand man was the tireless organizer Ralph Abernathy, pastor of the First Baptist Church in Montgomery. He helped turn King's oratory into effective action, and was arrested with King 19 times.

In 1956, Rustin proposed the expansion of the Montgomery Movement to cities across the South. The next year, King and Abernathy invited 60 ministers to Atlanta, and formed the Southern Christian Leadership Conference.

Eisenhower's motto was "Send in the Army." In 1957, he ordered the 101st Airborne to guard nine black students newly enrolled in Central High in Little Rock, Arkansas.

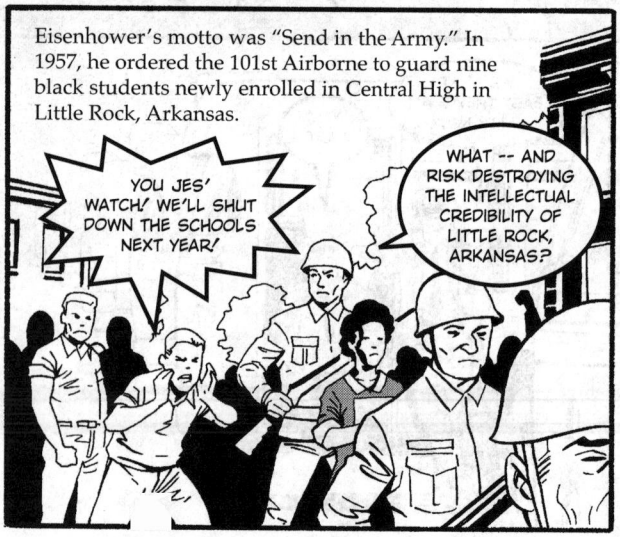

In 1958, black students began a "sit-in" at the Dockum Drugs lunch counter in Wichita, Kansas. The tactic spread to Oklahoma City in 1959, and to Greensboro, North Carolina in 1960. From Greensboro it went national, targeting a dozen cities at once.

Divinity student John Lewis ran sit-ins in Nashville; by the age of 23, he had been arrested 24 times. At 21, he helped organize – and rode in – the first Freedom Ride.
I THOUGHT I SAW DEATH, BUT NOTHING CAN MAKE ME QUESTION THE PHILOSOPHY OF NONVIOLENCE.
In 1961, the "Freedom Rides" combined the proven tactics of sitting and buses. The 436 Freedom Riders – mostly young black students – rode into segregated cities to pit Jim Crow laws at bus stations against the 1960 Supreme Court ruling requiring integration of interstate bus transportation.
THESE ANIMALS HAVE NO RESPECT FOR THE LAW.
I KNOW. AND ONCE THE KLAN FINISHES WITH THEM, I'LL GO ARREST THEM.
With a local minister, Fred Shuttlesworth, the SCLC planned a mass action in Birmingham, Alabama to boycott and protest downtown over the Easter shopping season. On Good Friday, 1963, King was arrested for violating an injunction and jailed for eight days.
Injustice anywhere is a threat to justice everywhere. We are caught in an inescapable network of mutuality, tied in a single garment of destiny. Whatever affects one directly, affects all indirectly. ... Anyone who lives inside the United States can never be considered an outsider anywhere within its bounds.

On May 2, the SCLC agreed to let 1,000 schoolchildren join protesters in marches downtown. Public Safety Commissioner "Bull" Connor met the marchers with firehoses and police dogs. But by May 10, with 2,500 protesters overfilling the jail and 3,000 more on the streets, Birmingham caved and desegregated.

The Kennedy administration was initially cool to the Movement and tried to have it both ways. But the spectacle of Birmingham – climaxing with a church bombing by the KKK in September that killed four little girls – forced Kennedy's hand.

The Movement kept the pressure on Kennedy and Congress through the summer. A. Philip Randolph, the head of the Brotherhood of Pullman Sleeping Car Porters and vice president of the AFL-CIO, resurrected his 1941 plan for a vast march on Washington. His union skills and Rustin's administrative genius put together a program that allied the SCLC with the NAACP, CORE, the Urban League, and the SNCC. Eventually, 250,000 people marched.

EVEN THOUGH WE FACE THE DIFFICULTIES OF TODAY AND TOMORROW, I STILL HAVE A DREAM. IT IS A DREAM DEEPLY ROOTED IN THE AMERICAN DREAM.
I HAVE A DREAM THAT ONE DAY THIS NATION WILL RISE UP AND LIVE OUT THE TRUE MEANING OF ITS CREED: "WE HOLD THESE TRUTHS TO BE SELF-EVIDENT, THAT ALL MEN ARE CREATED EQUAL.
I HAVE A DREAM THAT ONE DAY ON THE RED HILLS OF GEORGIA, THE SONS OF FORMER SLAVES AND THE SONS OF FORMER SLAVE OWNERS WILL BE ABLE TO SIT DOWN TOGETHER AT THE TABLE OF BROTHERHOOD.
I HAVE A DREAM THAT ONE DAY EVEN THE STATE OF MISSISSIPPI, A STATE SWELTERING WITH THE HEAT OF INJUSTICE, SWELTERING WITH THE HEAT OF OPPRESSION, WILL BE TRANSFORMED INTO AN OASIS OF FREEDOM AND JUSTICE
I HAVE A DREAM THAT MY FOUR LITTLE CHILDREN WILL ONE DAY LIVE IN A NATION WHERE THEY WILL NOT BE JUDGED BY THE COLOR OF THEIR SKIN BUT BY THE CONTENT OF THEIR CHARACTER. ...
... AND WHEN THIS HAPPENS, WHEN WE ALLOW FREEDOM TO RING, WHEN WE LET IT RING FROM EVERY VILLAGE AND EVERY HAMLET, FROM EVERY STATE AND EVERY CITY, WE WILL BE ABLE TO SPEED UP THAT DAY WHEN ALL OF GOD'S CHILDREN, BLACK MEN AND WHITE MEN, JEWS AND GENTILES, PROTESTANTS AND CATHOLICS, WILL BE ABLE TO JOIN HANDS AND SING IN THE WORDS OF THE OLD NEGRO SPIRITUAL:
FREE AT LAST! FREE AT LAST!
THANK GOD ALMIGHTY, WE ARE FREE AT LAST!
On August 28, 1963, Martin Luther King called in Lincoln's promissory note.

WE PREACH FREEDOM AROUND THE WORLD, AND WE MEAN IT, AND WE CHERISH OUR FREEDOM HERE AT HOME, BUT ARE WE TO SAY TO THE WORLD AND, MUCH MORE IMPORTANTLY, TO EACH OTHER THAT THIS IS A LAND OF THE FREE EXCEPT FOR THE NEGROES; THAT WE HAVE NO SECOND-CLASS CITIZENS EXCEPT NEGROES; THAT WE HAVE NO CLASS OR CASTE SYSTEM, NO GHETTOS, NO MASTER RACE EXCEPT WITH RESPECT TO NEGROES?
President Kennedy had finally made his own civil rights speech on June 11.
His proposed Civil Rights Act languished in Congress until his successor, President Johnson, forced it through in 1964.
SAY IT! SEGREGATION IN PUBLIC ACCOMMODATION ...
OWWW! ... AND BY STATE AND FEDERAL GOVERNMENTS ... OWW!
... AND EMPLOYMENT DISCRIMINATION ...
OWWW!... ARE ILLEGAL! OWWW!
On March 7, 1965, 600 marchers – led by John Lewis and including Rosa Parks – attempted to cross Edmund Pettus Bridge outside Selma, Alabama, on their way to Montgomery to present a petition to Governor Wallace. State troopers and county sheriffs attacked them with clubs, bullwhips, and tear gas, injuring 50 protesters.
Although the Twenty-fourth Amendment, ratified in 1964, prohibited poll taxes ...
BALLOT
TO ENSURE SERVICE
... it was not until Johnson's Voting Rights Act in 1965 that the federal government prohibited discrimination at the voting booth, and enforced federal remedies in such cases. A century later, Reconstruction was again the law of the land.

Why was this Movement successful, when previous civil rights campaigns had ultimately failed?
Part of it was the timing. The Movement started just after a war against two murderously racist empires, and just at the beginning of a new religious revival in white America.
THERE IS NO SCRIPTURAL BASIS FOR SEGREGATION. ... THE GROUND AT THE FOOT OF THE CROSS IS LEVEL, AND IT TOUCHES MY HEART WHEN I SEE WHITES STANDING SHOULDER TO SHOULDER WITH BLACKS AT THE CROSS.
Part of it was a constellation of talent and guts unprecedented in American life since the Founding Fathers.
And part of it was David Sarnoff's decision, in 1928, to fund the research of Vladimir Zworykin, and keep pouring RCA money into his invention for the next decade.
I CAN HAVE A WORKING TUBE FOR YOU IN TWO YEARS FOR $ 50,000 ... NOT INCLUDING THE $ 1,000,000 TO PAY PHILO FARNSWORTH, WHO ACTUALLY INVENTED IT LAST YEAR.
Because seeing something on television isn't the same as reading about it.
THEY'VE JUST TURNED DOGS ON THE PROTESTERS HERE IN BIRMINGHAM ... POLICE DOGS LUNGING AT PEOPLE ...
The revolution was, in fact, televised.

So what did President Eisenhower do when he wasn't desegregating schools in Little Rock?
WOK
I CALL IT "DYNAMIC CONSERVATISM."
By "dynamically" ignoring McCarthy, Eisenhower let him overreach. McCarthy accused George Marshall of being a Communist, and foolishly investigated the Army. In 1954, the Army's lawyer demolished him on television.
HAVE YOU NO SENSE OF DECENCY, SIR, AT LONG LAST? HAVE YOU LEFT NO SENSE OF DECENCY?
Eisenhower's America vanquished another crippling infection in 1954, when Jonas Salk developed a vaccine against polio, ending a childhood nightmare forever.
Two giants of American cartooning helped redefine American childhood in their own ways, whether by drawing the darkly psychological …
PSYCHIATRIC HELP 5¢
THE DOCTOR IS IN
… or building the "happiest place on Earth."

How America lived was changing. The GI Bill made suburbs affordable …
LEVITTOWN New Ranch House Style for 1949 From $7,990
… and "white flight" filled them fast.
WHEW!
Americans bought 60 million cars during the 1950s. Eisenhower signed the National Interstate and Defense Highways Act in 1956 to relieve congestion and improve defense planning. The interstates also helped give America fast food, chain motels, and unprecedented social mobility.
McDonald's HAMBURGERS
Established 1954 Over 12 Served!
By contrast, beginning with the 1949 Housing Act, "urban renewal" knocked down more housing than it built and by 1973 had displaced one million Americans – two-thirds of them black. Public housing became a trap, and then a prison, for the next 30 years.

America's changing lifestyle churned up increasing cultural turmoil in the 1950s. Malcolm X revived black nationalism when he became the Nation of Islam's public face in 1954.
SITTING AT THE TABLE DOESN'T MAKE YOU A DINER, UNLESS YOU EAT SOME OF WHAT'S ON THAT PLATE. BEING HERE IN AMERICA DOESN'T MAKE YOU AN AMERICAN.
Miles Davis and John Coltrane revived jazz, blending bebop with melody.
Something, someone, some spirit was pursuing all of us across the desert of life and was bound to catch us before we reached heaven.
The Beat Generation tried to rebuild American letters.
John Ford looked into the abyss from the high-water mark of the Western.
THAT'LL BE THE DAY.
Television, America's newest art form, was inventing itself – from *Dragnet* to *I Love Lucy* – and rebelling against itself at the same time.
The TWILIGHT ZONE
TONIGHT ON THE NEWS: PRESIDENT EISENHOWER SENDS MORE ADVISERS TO VIETNAM.
And the blues had a baby, and they named it rock and roll.

Overseas, things were in turmoil, too. Both the United States and the Soviets tested hydrogen bombs, which ruled out open warfare between the superpowers.
So covert warfare took over. The CIA knocked over socialist governments in Iran (1953) and Guatemala (1954).

Stalin died in 1952, and the Soviets got a new leader, Nikita Khrushchev.
WE WILL BURY YOU.

In 1956, Soviet troops crushed rebellions in Poland and Hungary …
RIGHT AFTER WE FINISH BURYING EASTERN EUROPE, AGAIN.

… while the United States looked on helplessly.
AH, WHEN WE URGED EASTERN EUROPE TO RISE UP AGAINST THEIR SOVIET MASTERS, WE, ER, HAD MORE IN MIND SOMETHING ALONG THE LINES OF, AH, A STINGINGLY SATIRICAL PLAY. EVEN A SERIES OF PLAYS.

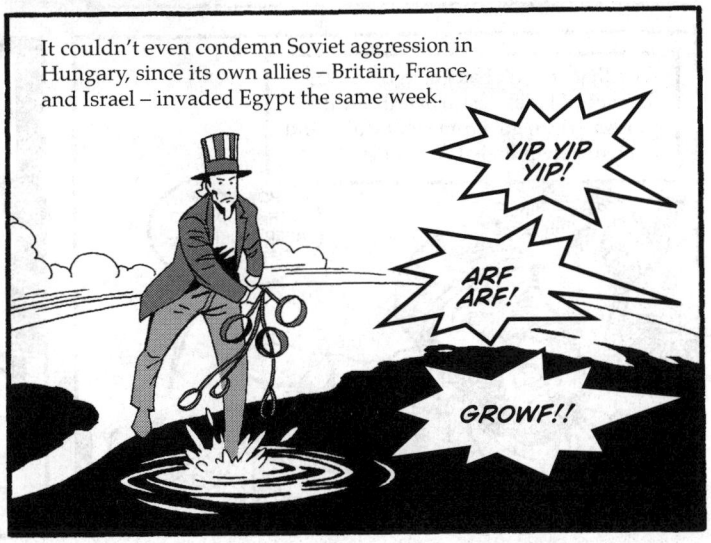
It couldn't even condemn Soviet aggression in Hungary, since its own allies – Britain, France, and Israel – invaded Egypt the same week.
YIP YIP YIP!
ARF ARF!
GROWF!!

On October 4, 1957, the Soviets launched Sputnik, the first artificial satellite. It didn't take a rocket scientist to see the implications.
BEEP
-- WE WILL BURY YOU --
BEEP
-- WE WILL BURY YOU --
BEEP
The U.S. soon caught up, launching Explorer I two months later – and more to the point, building its own ICBM force up from scratch.
ALL IT TAKES IS A LITTLE GERMAN SUPERIORITY ... ER, I MEAN YANKEE KNOW-HOW.
Democrats – and U.S. aerospace companies – made hay over the imaginary "missile gap." To settle the question, the CIA launched U-2 spy plane flights over Russia.
THAT'S IT ... NOW GIVE ME SOME ANGER ... YOU'RE BEAUTIFUL, BABY ... JUST LIKE THAT ... NOW HOLD IT ...
Which proved embarrassing when the Soviets shot down and captured the U-2 pilot Francis Gary Powers – two weeks before a summit meeting between Eisenhower and Khrushchev.
PERFECT! ... NOW LOOK ANGRY ... NOW LOOK EMBARRASSED ...
As if that weren't bad enough, in 1959 the radical Fidel Castro overthrew the pro-American government of Cuba, and immediately pursued Soviet ties.
HOW LONG IS HE GOING TO KEEP TALKING -- FIFTY YEARS?
Such crises notwithstanding, Eisenhower would easily have won a third term in 1960 – if the Twenty-second Amendment back in 1951 hadn't set a two-term presidential limit.
AND I WOULD LIKE TO ASSURE MY REPUBLICAN COLLEAGUES THAT THIS PROPOSED AMENDMENT WILL ABSOLUTELY GUARANTEE THAT FRANKLIN D. ROOSEVELT WILL NEVER RISE FROM THE DEAD TO TERRORIZE US AGAIN.
HEAR, HEAR!

Instead, Eisenhower's vice president, Richard Nixon, ran against the Democratic senator from Massachusetts, John F. Kennedy.

Thanks to his running mate, Senator "Landslide" Lyndon Johnson of Texas – and to the Chicago machine boss Richard J. Daley – Kennedy defeated Nixon after a squeaker election.
SO THAT'S HOW THE GAME IS PLAYED, EH?

Kennedy recognized the symbolic importance of the "Space Race." After Soviet cosmonaut Yuri Gagarin became the first man in space, Kennedy doubled down.
I BELIEVE THAT THIS NATION SHOULD COMMIT ITSELF TO ACHIEVING THE GOAL, BEFORE THIS DECADE IS OUT, OF LANDING A MAN ON THE MOON AND RETURNING HIM BACK SAFELY TO THE EARTH.
NO SINGLE SPACE PROJECT IN THIS PERIOD WILL BE MORE IMPRESSIVE TO MANKIND, OR MORE IMPORTANT FOR THE LONG-RANGE EXPLORATION OF SPACE; AND NONE WILL BE SO DIFFICULT OR EXPENSIVE TO ACCOMPLISH.

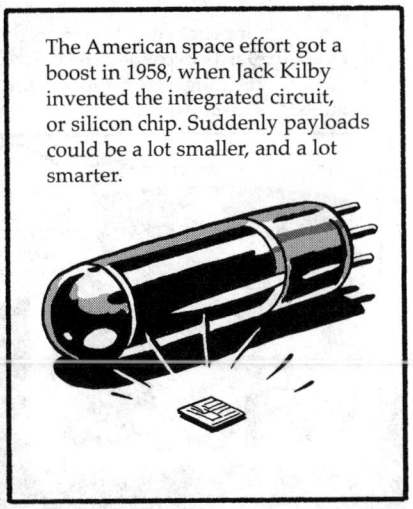
The American space effort got a boost in 1958, when Jack Kilby invented the integrated circuit, or silicon chip. Suddenly payloads could be a lot smaller, and a lot smarter.

For instance, the United States launched the first communications satellite, Telstar, in 1962.
This can't end well.
JED NAMED A MAN 'BOUT STORY A LITTLE HERE'S
POOR MOUNTAINEER BARELY KEPT HIS FAMILY FED

Other parts of the future started coming true:
Theodore H. Maiman built the first working laser in 1960.

And in even better news, William House invented the cochlear implant for the deaf in 1961.
POOR MOUNTAINEER BARELY KEPT HIS FAMILY FED.
TAKE IT BACK OUT.

In April of 1961, Kennedy approved a CIA invasion of Cuba, but refused to provide U.S. air or naval support. This "Bay of Pigs" failure sealed Castro's domination of the island. By 1962, 200,000 Cubans had fled to America; another 300,000 would join them in the next decade.

A similarly embarrassing exodus from East Germany to West Berlin drove the Communists to erect the Berlin Wall in August 1961. Kennedy allowed the wall to stand, but made good propaganda from a bad situation with a fiery oration in now-isolated West Berlin.

ALL FREE MEN, WHEREVER THEY MAY LIVE, ARE CITIZENS OF BERLIN, AND, THEREFORE, AS A FREE MAN, I TAKE PRIDE IN THE WORDS "ICH BIN EIN BERLINER."

Looking for better covert warriors than the CIA, Kennedy vastly expanded the U.S. Army Special Forces, launching a PR campaign for the newly dubbed "Green Berets."

WITH THIS DEPLOYMENT, PRESIDENT KENNEDY HAS INCREASED AMERICAN TROOP STRENGTH IN VIETNAM TO 16,000 ADVISERS ...

Kennedy also sent bright young people overseas for other reasons; his Peace Corps attracted over 7,000 idealistic volunteers in its first two years.

In the 1960s, perhaps the most effective American aid program ever began to bear fruit: the "Green Revolution." Beginning in 1944, the agronomist Norman Borlaug developed higher-yield grain cultivars that helped make Mexico self-sufficient in wheat by 1963, Pakistan likewise by 1968, and India self-sufficient in all cereals by 1974. Worldwide, the "Green Revolution" may have saved over a billion people from starvation.

WE WILL BE GUILTY OF CRIMINAL NEGLIGENCE, WITHOUT EXTENUATION, IF WE PERMIT FUTURE FAMINES.

In June 1962, Khrushchev decided to insert Soviet medium-range nuclear missiles into Cuba.
THERE SEEM TO BE AN AWFUL LOT OF NUCLEAR MISSILES IN THIS CIGAR FACTORY.
MAYBE THEY'RE JUST REALLY BIG CIGARS.
On October 14, the United States noticed.
On October 22, Kennedy ordered a blockade of Cuba.
CUBA
END THE BLOCKADE AND PROMISE NOT TO INVADE CUBA, AND WE'LL WITHDRAW THE MISSILES.
THE LAST THING I NEED IS ANOTHER INVASION OF CUBA.
AND WITHDRAW YOUR MISSILES FROM TURKEY.
I CAN'T DO THAT! THE PRESS WOULD CRUCIFY ME.
I WON'T TELL IF YOU DON'T.
DEAL.
On October 28, Khrushchev and Kennedy worked out a deal, and the Cuban Missile Crisis was averted.
The crisis had two major outcomes: Khrushchev looked weak, and fell from power two years later.
HOW COULD YOU ENDANGER THE REVOLUTION WITH YOUR RECKLESS ADVENTURISM?
HOW COULD YOU BETRAY THE REVOLUTION WITH YOUR COWARDLY RETREAT?
And the Pentagon started paying attention to two obscure ideas developed that year by a RAND Corporation researcher named Paul Baran: distributed communications networks, and packet-switching. Both would be crucial for nuclear war-fighting … or, as it turned out, for interlinking computers.
I THINK THIS *RAND* REPORT IS THE KEY TO COMMAND AND CONTROL DURING A NUCLEAR WAR.
IF IT COULD ONLY HELP ME SELL MY HULA HOOP COLLECTION TO COMPLETE STRANGERS, IT WOULD BE PERFECT.

Vietnam wasn't going Kennedy's way either. Although South Vietnamese President Ngo Dinh Diem was winning his war against the Vietcong communist rebels, he was embarrassingly brutal about it.
So Kennedy approved a November 1, 1963, CIA-backed coup against Diem that wound up being even more embarrassingly brutal.
SO YOU'RE TELLING ME THAT DIEM COMMITTED SUICIDE ... IN A CATHOLIC CHURCH ... BY STABBING HIMSELF ... AND SHOOTING HIMSELF WITH A RIFLE ... REPEATEDLY ... WITH HIS HANDS TIED BEHIND HIM.
YOU KNOW, I DID GO TO HARVARD.
Three weeks later, President Kennedy was shot and killed in Dallas by a low-rent agitator named Lee Harvey Oswald.
Vice President Lyndon Johnson became president, and demolished Republican Senator Barry Goldwater in the 1964 election.
WE ARE NOT ABOUT TO SEND AMERICAN BOYS NINE TO TEN THOUSAND MILES AWAY FROM HOME TO DO WHAT ASIAN BOYS OUGHT TO BE DOING FOR THEMSELVES.
AS I HAVE REPEATEDLY MADE CLEAR, THE UNITED STATES INTENDS NO RASHNESS, AND SEEKS NO WIDER WAR.
WE MUST MAKE IT CLEAR TO ALL THAT THE UNITED STATES IS UNITED IN ITS DETERMINATION TO BRING ABOUT THE END OF COMMUNIST SUBVERSION AND AGGRESSION IN THE AREA ... I RECOMMEND A RESOLUTION EXPRESSING THE SUPPORT OF THE CONGRESS FOR ALL NECESSARY ACTION TO PROTECT OUR ARMED FORCES AND TO ASSIST NATIONS COVERED BY THE SEATO TREATY.
Three months before the election, Congress wrote Johnson a blank check for war in Vietnam.

Congress was writing a lot of blank checks then. Using his three decades of legislative experience to good effect, Johnson pushed through a series of bills he hoped would build the "Great Society."

IT'S ALL AMMO FOR THE *WAR ON POVERTY.*

I HOPE IT GOES AS WELL AS YOUR OTHER WAR.

MASS TRANSIT ACT

CHILD SAFETY ACT

ENDANGERED SPECIES ACT

NATIONAL ENDOWMENT FOR THE ARTS

ELEMENTARY AND SECONDARY EDUCATION ACT

FOOD STAMPS

HEAD START

WATER QUALITY ACT

MEDICAID

MEDICARE

Johnson's Civil Rights Act of 1964 also banned employment discrimination against women, who went from 33% of the workforce in 1950 to 43% in 1970.

Johnson reopened the golden door with the Hart-Celler Act of 1965, which abolished the restrictive national quota system and allowed unlimited "family reunification." Within 20 years, annual immigration totals more than doubled. Immigrants increasingly came from Asia, Latin America, and the Caribbean rather than Europe.

ADOBO

PIEROGI

ROPA VIEJA

BURRITOS

PHO

The 1960s (and 1970s) saw the biggest youth movements since the 1820s (and 1830s). The median age actually dropped from 29.5 in 1960 to 28 in 1970. The 76 million kids born between 1946 and 1964 made up a "Baby Boom" of epic proportions. The birth control pill, approved in 1960, ended the Boom …
… and brought the "sexual revolution" to the Boomers.
GIRLS SAY YES TO GUYS WHO SAY NO
Rock and roll shortened its name to "rock," and got all serious.
Drug use blossomed; LSD moved from psychiatry to the counterculture, and marijuana use likely increased by 1000% from 1962 to 1967.
EIGHT MILES HIGH AND WHEN YOU TOUCH DOWN YOU'LL FIND THAT IT'S STRANGER THAN KNOWN
In 1967, 100,000 young people swarmed into San Francisco for the "Summer of Love," which broadcast – and marketed – the hippie lifestyle to all America.
Youth politics radicalized – on all sides.
WALLACE '68
The Sixties climaxed with the music festival at Woodstock, New York in August of 1969, and ended with a fatal stabbing at the Altamont Music Festival four months later.
AFTER ALL, WHEN THE LAST BABY BOOM TOOK OVER, EVERYTHING WORKED OUT.
DON'T TRUST ANYONE BORN AFTER 1830!
After three years of increasing agitation, the Twenty-sixth Amendment was ratified in 1971, lowering the national voting age to 18.

Q: What is the best weapon to use against this target?
In February of 1965, in order to halt infiltration of North Vietnamese aid and cadres into South Vietnam along the "Ho Chi Minh Trail," President Johnson and Secretary of Defense Robert McNamara decided on …

A: If you said "bombing raids from 30,000 feet," then YOU are one of "the best and the brightest!"
… a bombing campaign, Operation Rolling Thunder.

Johnson and McNamara personally micro-managed the air war. Slow escalation allowed Soviet and Chinese aid to North Vietnam to keep pace with American attacks.
DON'T WORRY, MR. PRESIDENT -- WE'LL STOP THIS INFILTRATION SCIENTIFICALLY. JUST LIKE I STOPPED THE EDSEL WHEN I WAS AT FORD.
DIDN'T YOU TAKE THREE YEARS TO STOP THE EDSEL?
THIS CAN'T END WELL.

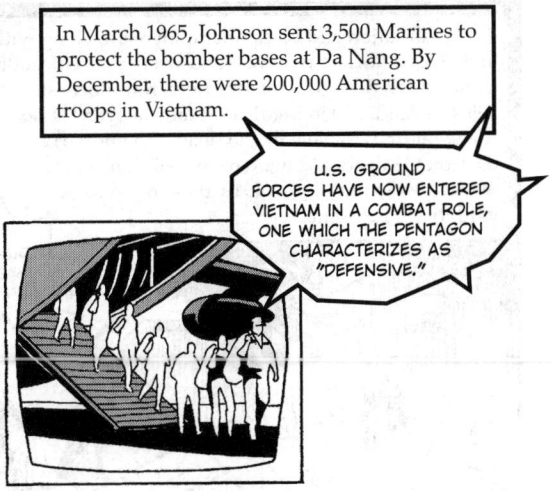
In March 1965, Johnson sent 3,500 Marines to protect the bomber bases at Da Nang. By December, there were 200,000 American troops in Vietnam.
U.S. GROUND FORCES HAVE NOW ENTERED VIETNAM IN A COMBAT ROLE, ONE WHICH THE PENTAGON CHARACTERIZES AS "DEFENSIVE."

Protests against the war began with protests against the draft. By 1973, over half a million inductees would dodge the draft, compared with about 373,000 draft evaders in WWII, and 448,000 in WWI.
WHAT ARE YOU BURNING?
MY DRAFT CARD, TO PROTEST THIS UNJUST WAR!
DON'T YOU HAVE A STUDENT DEFERMENT ANYWAY?
I DO! PRETTY UNJUST, HUH?

In a precursor of things to come, outspoken war opponent Malcolm X – who had broken with the Nation of Islam in 1964 – was assassinated by three Black Muslims on February 21, 1965.

Not all of Johnson's wars went astray. In April 1965, he landed marines in the Dominican Republic to bolster the anti-socialist side in a burgeoning civil war. Seventeen months (and 13 American fatalities) later, the Americans withdrew, leaving behind a stable right-wing government.

I SAY AGAIN, I SEE NO PIGS. NO PIGS IN THIS BAY.

Anti-war protest hit the big time in 1967, with 400,000 people marching in New York City in August and 100,000 in Washington in October. Regardless, "hawks" outnumbered "doves" in a Gallup poll that winter, 52% to 35%.

DEMON, COME OUT!

IÄ! YOG-SOHOTH!

U.S. PENTAGON

Rising inflation and black unemployment, along with misguided "urban renewal" and white police brutality, contributed to a string of race riots from Rochester in 1964 (4 dead, 350 injured) and Watts in 1965 (34 dead, 1,072 injured) to Newark (26 dead, 725 injured) and Detroit (43 dead, 467 injured) in 1967. Unlike the white-instigated riots of 1919, these often began with black resistance.

BURN, BABY, BURN!!!

LONG HOT SUMMER

In 1968, on Tet (the Vietnamese New Year), cities burned in South Vietnam in a last-ditch Vietcong offensive ending in military disaster. The Vietcong and North Vietnamese army lost 100,000 fighters and retreated into the border zones.

DID YOU HEAR? GENERAL WESTMORELAND SAID "THE ENEMY IS UNABLE TO MOUNT A MAJOR OFFENSIVE."

THAT MUST BE WHY THEY SIMULTANEOUSLY LAUNCHED *114* MINOR OFFENSIVES INSTEAD.

Unfortunately, General William Westmoreland's unwarranted optimism and McNamara's incrementalism had eroded both the media's and the public's faith in Johnson's war. Tet was a victory too late; the President dropped out of the 1968 campaign in March.

TO SAY THAT WE ARE CLOSER TO VICTORY TODAY IS TO BELIEVE, IN THE FACE OF THE EVIDENCE, THE OPTIMISTS WHO HAVE BEEN WRONG IN THE PAST.

TO SUGGEST WE ARE ON THE EDGE OF DEFEAT IS TO YIELD TO UNREASONABLE PESSIMISM.

TO SAY THAT WE ARE MIRED IN STALEMATE SEEMS THE ONLY REALISTIC, YET UNSATISFACTORY, CONCLUSION.

Coincidentally, that month marked a turning point in another seemingly unending struggle. Cesar Chavez, founder of the United Farm Workers, went on a 28-day hunger strike to draw attention to a grape-pickers' strike that had also ground on since 1965. The growers signed a union contract the next year.
BECAUSE WE HAVE SUFFERED -- AND ARE NOT AFRAID TO SUFFER -- IN ORDER TO SURVIVE, WE ARE READY TO GIVE UP EVERYTHING, EVEN OUR LIVES ...
Chavez' model for political action, Dr. Martin Luther King Jr., went to Memphis, Tennessee, to support another strike, by sanitation workers.
On April 4, 1968, a sniper killed Dr. King there.
When he heard the news, presidential candidate Robert F. Kennedy, campaigning in Indianapolis, gave an impromptu speech to a black audience. Riots erupted in 60 cities across the country – but not in Indianapolis.
LET US DEDICATE OURSELVES TO WHAT THE GREEKS WROTE SO MANY YEARS AGO: TO TAME THE SAVAGENESS OF MAN AND MAKE GENTLE THE LIFE OF THIS WORLD.
LET US DEDICATE OURSELVES TO THAT, AND SAY A PRAYER FOR OUR COUNTRY AND FOR OUR PEOPLE.
On June 5, the night he won the California primary, Kennedy was shot and killed by Sirhan Sirhan, a deranged Palestinian.
The 1968 Democratic National Convention in Chicago wound up nominating Hubert Humphrey amid a "police riot" sparked when the Chicago Police Department clamped down on 10,000 anti-war protesters in Grant Park.
THE WHOLE WORLD IS WATCHING!
AND NOW IT'S GOING TO VOTE REPUBLICAN.
Riots at Columbia, Berkeley, and other universities accomplished little ... except to vault anti-protest politicians like California governor Ronald Reagan into national prominence.
DISSENT MUST STOP SHORT OF INTERFERING WITH THE RIGHTS OF OTHER INDIVIDUALS.

The Republican candidate in 1968, Richard Nixon, promised that "new leadership would end the war." Humphrey accused Nixon of having a "secret plan" to end the war …
VOTE NIX
I HAVE NO SECRET PLAN, BUT IF I DID, I COULD NOT REVEAL IT, LEST I ACCIDENTALLY DERAIL THE ONGOING PEACE TALKS.
… but actually, the only secret plan was President Johnson's.
BY AN ODD COINCIDENCE, I HAVE DECIDED TO HALT ALL BOMBING OF NORTH VIETNAM TODAY, THE THURSDAY BEFORE THE ELECTION.
A Harvard professor named Henry Kissinger, who served as a go-between in the Paris Peace Talks, tipped Nixon off. Nixon's own go-betweens convinced the South Vietnamese government to derail the peace talks until the election …
AND IT ISN'T VERY SECRET.
… which Nixon won, despite the segregationist George Wallace draining some of Nixon's "law and order" support to his third-party candidacy. By yet another odd coincidence, Henry Kissinger became Nixon's National Security Adviser.
HENRY, AS A HISTORIAN, WOULD YOU CALL THIS A CORRUPT BARGAIN, OR MORE OF A GRAND COMPROMISE?
After derailing Johnson's peace plan, President of South Vietnam Nguyen Van Thieu instituted a land reform program in 1970 that finally marginalized the Vietcong.
EVERY PEASANT IS ENTITLED TO 15 HECTARES OF LAND, AND TO ANY AND ALL UNEXPLODED LAND MINES HE MAY FIND ON IT.
Nixon's actual plan to end the war was a combination of increased bombing and "Vietnamization" – turning major combat operations over to the South Vietnamese army.
HEY, WE'RE PRETTY VIETNAMIZED ALREADY, MAN.

Nixon's domestic agenda would have seemed liberal indeed in 1960 – or 1980, for that matter.
I CREATED THE *EPA* AND *OSHA*, IMPOSED WAGE AND PRICE CONTROLS AND AFFIRMATIVE ACTION, INDEXED SOCIAL SECURITY TO INFLATION, LOWERED THE SPEED LIMIT, AND CREATED SUPPLEMENTAL SECURITY INCOME.
Nixon's cabinet task force on school integration completed much of Eisenhower's work, however. By facilitating unified school districts across the South, Nixon integrated 2 million black schoolchildren.
MY DAD *HATES* NIXON NOW.
MY DAD *ALWAYS* HATED NIXON.
Women's Liberation gathered steam … but no smoke! … during protests at the Miss America pageants in 1968 and 1969. By 1970, less than half of American women were full-time homemakers.
Miss America Pageant
Miss America Pageant
NO MORE MISS AMERICA
I THOUGHT WE WERE GOING TO BURN THOSE THINGS.
NO MORE BEAUTY STANDARDS
WE COULDN'T GET A PERMIT.
WELCOME TO THE CATTLE AUCTIO
FREEDOM TRASH CAN
WAY TO STICK IT TO THE MAN, ROBIN.
Gay liberation came out of the closet and onto the streets in 1969 during a riot over the closing of the Stonewall Inn in New York City.
STONEWALL INN
IT'S JUST LIKE THE *BOSTON MASSACRE!* I FEEL LIKE PAUL REVERE!
I'LL BET YOU DO, SUGAR.
And just possibly the most important change of 1969 hit on November 21, when the first truly interlinked computer system, the ARPANET, went live with four machines.
LO

But the Apollo 11 Moon landing got all the press. On July 20, 1969, Neil Armstrong became the first human being to set foot on another world.
THAT'S ONE SMALL STEP FOR A MAN -- ONE GIANT LEAP FOR MANKIND.
"I'll tell you, if there ever was a fragile-appearing piece of blue in space, it's the Earth right now."
– Astronaut Harrison Schmitt during Apollo 17, December 7, 1972.
The space program produced a lot of spinoffs. Its most unexpected side-effect may have been the way it supercharged the environmental movement. Seeing the Earth as a whole provided both symbol and incentive for the burgeoning campaigns to clean up pollution, protect endangered species and ecosystems, and generally re-assess human relations with the natural world.

On April 30, 1970, Nixon announced that the United States and South Vietnam were invading Cambodia in order to destroy North Vietnamese supply bases.

THIS IS NOT AN INVASION OF CAMBODIA.

The invasion damaged the American war effort more than it did the North Vietnamese: radicals bombed or burned 30 ROTC buildings and campus protest exploded again. At Kent State and Jackson State, National Guard and police fired on protesters, killing six.

Former State Department official Daniel Ellsberg leaked 7,000 pages of top secret Johnson Administration Vietnam documents to the *New York Times;* in a 6-3 decision, the Supreme Court upheld the legality of publishing them.

Other government papers vanished entirely in 1972 when the "national liberationist" American Indian Movement occupied the Bureau of Indian Affairs building in Washington.

HEY, ACCORDING TO THIS, WILLIAM HENRY HARRISON LIED ABOUT HIS BODY COUNTS, TOO!

In 1971 and 1972, Nixon moved to improve relations with the Soviets – the "détente" policy – and with their bitter rivals, the Communist Chinese.

I SEE YOU HAVE KILLED SIX PROTESTERS. ONLY *59,999,994* MORE AND YOU'LL BEAT MY RECORD.

DON'T TEMPT ME.

With Soviet and Chinese aid lessening, North Vietnam gambled on a major invasion of South Vietnam on Easter of 1972; American bombing stopped it dead.

Nixon steamrolled over Democratic Senator George McGovern in 1972, winning the second biggest landslide in American history.
YOU LIKE ME! YOU REALLY LIKE ME!

In January 1973, the draft ended.
NO WAR

So did America's part in the Vietnam War. 58,209 U.S. combat troops had been killed in Vietnam by March 29, 1973, when the last of them left.
U.S. GROUND FORCES HAVE NOW LEFT SOUTH VIETNAM, A NATION THE STATE DEPARTMENT CHARACTERIZES AS "SECURE."

WHAT ARE WE GOING TO FIGHT OVER NOW?
STOP THE WAR!!
I SUPPORT THE PRESIDENT

Also in January, the Supreme Court ruled 7-2 in favor of the plaintiff in *Roe v. Wade*. Abortion was now a constitutional right.
A STATE CRIMINAL ABORTION STATUTE OF THE CURRENT TEXAS TYPE, THAT EXCEPTS FROM CRIMINALITY ONLY A LIFESAVING PROCEDURE ON BEHALF OF THE MOTHER, WITHOUT REGARD TO PREGNANCY STAGE AND WITHOUT RECOGNITION OF THE OTHER INTERESTS INVOLVED, IS VIOLATIVE OF THE ***DUE PROCESS CLAUSE*** OF THE FOURTEENTH AMENDMENT.

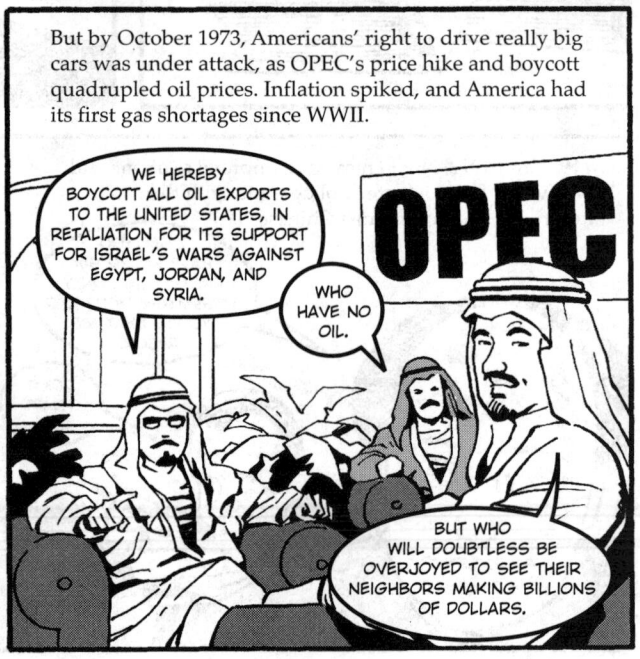
But by October 1973, Americans' right to drive really big cars was under attack, as OPEC's price hike and boycott quadrupled oil prices. Inflation spiked, and America had its first gas shortages since WWII.
WE HEREBY BOYCOTT ALL OIL EXPORTS TO THE UNITED STATES, IN RETALIATION FOR ITS SUPPORT FOR ISRAEL'S WARS AGAINST EGYPT, JORDAN, AND SYRIA.
OPEC
WHO HAVE NO OIL.
BUT WHO WILL DOUBTLESS BE OVERJOYED TO SEE THEIR NEIGHBORS MAKING BILLIONS OF DOLLARS.

But even as one great American industry was struggling, a new one was being born.
GM
Factory Closeout SALE
Three companies invented microprocessors between 1970 and 1973. One became the avionics for the F-14 Tomcat. One became a hand calculator.
And in 1974, one – the Intel 8080 -- became the guts of the first commercial personal computer, Edward Roberts' Altair 8800.
WHAT CAN IT DO? WHAT CAN'T IT DO? AFTER ONLY NINE HOURS OF FLIPPING TINY SWITCHES, YOU CAN TOTALLY CHANGE THE ORDER IN WHICH THESE LIGHTS BLINK!
In 1975, a young Harvard dropout, Bill Gates, got his start by selling software he hadn't written yet to the makers of the Altair.
I'M NOT SURE WHY THE SCREEN JUST TURNED BLUE LIKE THAT.
ESPECIALLY SINCE THAT'S A MONOCHROME MONITOR.
At Xerox' Palo Alto Research Center, their Alto computer had a mouse, a laser printer, a keyboard, software, and a color graphic user interface. In 1974. But no marketing plan.
GREAT NEWS! STANFORD HAS JUST AGREED TO ACCEPT ANOTHER 100 ALTOS FOR FREE!
HOT DOG!
A few miles away in Cupertino, California, hobbyists Steve Wozniak and Steve Jobs built the Apple I personal computer in 1976. The next year, their Apple II became the first successful home PC.
THIS IS GOING TO BE THE GREATEST THING EVER. IT WILL REVOLUTIONIZE THE WORLD.
CALM DOWN, STEVE, IT'S JUST A SODA.

In January 1973, seven Nixon re-election staffers were convicted of burglary and conspiracy for a break-in at Democratic National Committee headquarters in the Watergate Hotel.
WHY ARE WE DOING THIS, EXACTLY?
SO NIXON CAN BEAT GEORGE MCGOVERN IN NOVEMBER.
SEEMS LIKE GILDING THE LILY, IF YOU ASK ME.

One of the burglars fingered White House higher-ups: the presidential counsel, White House chief of staff, chief domestic policy adviser, and the former attorney general. All wound up doing time, as would half a dozen others.
YOU CAN'T PUT ME IN WITH THESE GUYS! YOU KNOW WHAT THEY DO TO SNITCHES ON THE INSIDE!

Congress and a special prosecutor began investigating the Watergate cover-up, and discovered the existence of a White House taping system that had been in place since FDR. When Nixon finally turned the tapes over to Congress, there was a mysterious 18½-minute gap … and hard evidence of the president committing conspiracy to obstruct justice.
YOU THINK THE THING TO DO IS TO GET THEM, THE FBI, TO STOP?
RIGHT, FINE.

In October, Vice President Spiro Agnew resigned after pleading "no contest" to charges of tax evasion, bribery, and money laundering. Nixon appointed congressman Gerald Ford vice president, under the Twenty-fifth Amendment.

The Watergate investigations, meanwhile, were turning up all manner of Nixon malfeasance: illegal wiretaps, slush funds, illicit campaign contributions, using the FBI and IRS against his "enemies list," and forgetting to pay taxes.
PEOPLE HAVE GOT TO KNOW WHETHER OR NOT THEIR PRESIDENT IS A CROOK. WELL, I'M NOT A CROOK. I'VE EARNED EVERYTHING I'VE GOT.

In late July 1974, the House Judiciary Committee passed three articles of impeachment against the president. Before the whole House could vote on them, Nixon resigned, on August 9, 1974.
TO LEAVE OFFICE BEFORE MY TERM IS COMPLETED IS ABHORRENT TO EVERY INSTINCT IN MY BODY. BUT AS PRESIDENT I MUST PUT THE INTERESTS OF AMERICA FIRST. AMERICA NEEDS A FULL-TIME PRESIDENT AND A FULL-TIME CONGRESS.

Vice President Gerald Ford became President, and one month later pardoned Nixon for any and all offenses that he "committed or may have committed or taken part in."
MY FELLOW AMERICANS, OUR LONG NATIONAL NIGHTMARE IS OVER.

Beginning in November 1974, North Vietnam violated the Paris Peace Accords and invaded the South. Congress refused to provide arms or aid to South Vietnam.
IT'S SOUTH VIETNAM ... THEY SAY THEY'RE BEING INVADED, AND THEY WANT US TO FULFILL OUR TREATY OBLIGATIONS.
GIVE THEM THE NUMBER FOR THE CHEROKEE NATION AND HANG UP.
The end was predictable. Saigon fell on April 30, 1975; with the evacuation of the U.S. Embassy, the last Americans left Vietnam.
The Communists immediately purged and "re-educated" millions in the South; about half a million died, including about 200,000 "boat people" refugees. From 1978, the United States gave some Vietnamese asylum; 245,000 had reached America by 1980, and another 530,000 by 2000.
President Ford lost a close election in 1976 to Democratic governor Jimmy Carter of Georgia.
THERE IS NO SOVIET DOMINATION OF EASTERN EUROPE AND THERE NEVER WILL BE UNDER A FORD ADMINISTRATION.
THANK YOU, LORD!
Carter began deregulating the airline, trucking, and rail industries. He was less successful at cutting spending.
I DON'T KNOW HOW THEY DO THINGS DOWN IN ATLANTA, MR. PRESIDENT, BUT UP HERE SPENDING GOVERNMENT MONEY KEEPS US IN OFFICE.
NO, THAT'S PRETTY MUCH HOW IT WORKS IN ATLANTA, TOO.
Carter also brokered a peace deal between Egypt and Israel, the 1978 Camp David Accords.

An attempt to rescue the hostages in Iran ended in a dust storm on April 25, 1980. So, to all intents and purposes, did the Carter presidency.

In 1980, Ronald Reagan swept into office on a Republican wave. It was the first defeat of an elected incumbent president since Herbert Hoover.

IT MIGHT BE WELL IF YOU ASK YOURSELF ARE YOU BETTER OFF THAN YOU WERE FOUR YEARS AGO?

IS IT EASIER FOR YOU TO GO AND BUY THINGS IN THE STORES THAN IT WAS FOUR YEARS AGO?

IS THERE MORE OR LESS UNEMPLOYMENT ... THAN THERE WAS FOUR YEARS AGO?

IS AMERICA AS RESPECTED THROUGHOUT THE WORLD AS IT WAS?

DO YOU FEEL THAT ... WE'RE AS STRONG AS WE WERE FOUR YEARS AGO?

Less than 70 days into his administration, an assassination attempt nearly succeeded in aborting the "Reagan Revolution." Instead, Reagan's wit under stress bought him a longer honeymoon with the American public.

I HOPE YOU'RE REPUBLICANS.

Reagan rapidly quashed an illegal strike by the air traffic controllers' union, PATCO, firing 11,345 strikers and accelerating the marginalization of American unions.

I *TOLD* YOU WE SHOULDN'T HAVE ENDORSED HIM.

Reagan revived JFK's policy of steep tax cuts to stimulate the economy, lowering the top bracket from 70% to 28%. Tax revenues increased, though not as fast as the deficit.

GOVERNMENT'S VIEW OF THE ECONOMY COULD BE SUMMED UP IN A FEW SHORT PHRASES: IF IT MOVES, TAX IT. IF IT KEEPS MOVING, REGULATE IT. AND IF IT STOPS MOVING, SUBSIDIZE IT.

Reagan accelerated Carter's deregulation moves, and supercharged Carter's defense buildup. Real defense spending increased by 50% during his first term.

ONCE YOU BUY THE FIRST THOUSAND, THEY GET REALLY AFFORDABLE.

Another Carter holdover, Federal Reserve Chairman Paul Volcker, spent three years choking off inflation. After a short but deep recession, the economy recovered completely. It more than recovered; the Long Boom that began in 1982 has so far tripled the U.S. economy in real terms with only two brief stalls.

Volcker's restraint may have contributed to the savings and loan crisis, by raising the price of money higher than S&L returns on mortgage loans. Congress drastically loosened regulations in an attempt to save the S&L industry, only to create a $200 billion mess when the S&Ls inevitably failed anyway in the late 1980s.
I KNOW A GUY SAVINGS & LOAN
EIGHT NATION SAVIN & LOAN PANCA HUT
NOT A MAFIA FRONT S & L
In the 1960s and 1970s, lawsuits made institutionalizing the mentally ill more difficult, federal law encouraged deinstitutionalization, and budget-cutters defunded expensive community treatment centers and public housing. This created a "perfect storm" of homelessness in the 1980s, exacerbated by disintegrating families in the inner cities.
IT'S ALL WROTE DOWN IN THE BOOK WE'RE LIVING IN!
WHAT DID HE SAY?
SOMETHING ABOUT UNINTENDED CONSEQUENCES OF WELL-MEANING LEGISLATION CAUSING THE HOMELESSNESS CRISIS.
OH, SO HE'S A NUT, THEN.
During the 1970s and 1980s, the primary consequence of the Nixon and Reagan "war on drugs" was to change drug-smuggling patterns from low-profit, high-volume marijuana to high-profit, low-volume cocaine. Drug use of all kinds increased throughout the era, despite Nancy Reagan's "Just Say No" campaign.
THIS MUST BE THAT "TRICKLE-DOWN ECONOMICS" I'VE HEARD SO MUCH ABOUT.
The emergence of the AIDS plague in the early 1980s radicalized the gay rights community. The activist Gay Men's Health Crisis founded in 1982 split with the militant ACT-UP in 1987, a year in which over 13,000 Americans died of AIDS.
SILENCE = DEATH
By contrast, the women's liberation movement suffered a major setback in 1982, when the Equal Rights Amendment failed ratification after 10 years.
A WOMAN NEEDS A MAN LIKE A FISH NEEDS A BICYCLE!
BUT THAT SAID, THREE MORE STATE LEGISLATURES WOULD BE NICE!!

In 1981, the space program got its own boost with the first space shuttle mission, beginning a decade of increased satellite deployment.

LOVE ♫ BOAT, ♪ SOON ♫ YOU'LL BE ♫ TAKING ♪ A RIDE

Satellite networks (and the deregulatory Cable Act of 1984) were crucial to the growth of cable TV, which blossomed from 16 million homes to 53 million in the 1980s. (Cell phones, invented by Martin Cooper at Motorola in 1973, likewise blossomed after the FCC authorized commercial cellular service.)

The IBM PC and Microsoft's DOS software became an overwhelming market alliance in 1981...

... and two years later, the U.S. Patent Office awarded the first ever software patent, for a spreadsheet. VisiCalc had meanwhile introduced the first major commercial spreadsheet in 1979, and the productivity boom had started.

HOW TO CALCULATE JUST HOW MUCH PRODUCTIVITY WE'LL ALL LOSE WHEN THE INTERNET GETS INVENTED...

On the Internet, the TCP/IP protocol became standard in 1983, boosting interoperability. During the 1980s, the number of computers on the Net went from 200 to 313,000.

!!!

New technologies saved lives, too. Invented separately by Paul Lauterbur and Raymond Damadian in the 1970s, the first commercial MRI machine appeared in an American hospital in 1980. A decade later, there were over 1,900 across the country.

HERE'S LOOKING AT ME, KID.

A more primitive technology, the truck bomb, destroyed the U.S. Embassy in Beirut on April 18, 1983, and then on October 23, the barracks of U.S. Marines in Lebanon to enforce a ceasefire. 258 Americans died in the two bombings; Reagan withdrew the American presence the next year.
Hezbollah, the Iranian-backed terrorist group responsible, carried out an ongoing campaign of kidnapping hostages as insurance against retaliation. From 1982 to 1988, Hezbollah took 25 Americans hostage; 10 were killed or died in captivity.
On October 25, 1983, Reagan took advantage of a coup on the Cuban-allied island of Grenada to invade the island and install a friendly democratic government. U.S. forces had more trouble staying out of each other's way than they did with the Cubans.
GOSH, I HOPE WE'LL ALL FIT.
GRENADA
Reagan also hugely expanded the Carter program of aid to the anti-Soviet mujahideen rebels in Afghanistan, from $20 million in 1980 to $630 million in 1987.
WHAT'S RUSSIAN FOR "VIETNAM," MAHMOUD?
The "Reagan Doctrine" covered more than Afghanistan. The United States provided covert aid to anti-Communist forces in Angola, Cambodia, and Nicaragua, and supported the anti-Communist government in the El Salvador civil war.
IT'S LIKE IT'S NOT SAFE TO INVADE PLACES ANY MORE.
Reagan didn't neglect Europe, either. Despite immense protests, the United States and NATO deployed advanced Pershing II and cruise missiles in Germany, Italy, and Britain, countering Soviet SS-20s and leveling the apocalyptic playing field once more.
NO WAR!
Mashine Brennt!
Hinter Uns Die Sintflut
ZUVIEL HITZE!

Rising prosperity and new Cold War toughness carried Reagan to a landslide re-election victory in 1984, carrying every state except Minnesota.

IT'S MORNING AGAIN IN AMERICA, AND UNDER THE LEADERSHIP OF PRESIDENT REAGAN, OUR COUNTRY IS PROUDER AND STRONGER AND BETTER. WHY WOULD WE EVER WANT TO RETURN TO WHERE WE WERE LESS THAN FOUR SHORT YEARS AGO?

Reagan's second term moved toward a post-Cold War world. In the Philippines, South Korea, and Chile, the United States backed democratic movements and encouraged the ouster of anti-American dictators.

MINE SAYS "GOOD LUCK ...

... ON YOUR RETIREMENT."

MINE, TOO.

The tenth mission of *Challenger,* the second space shuttle, started on January 28, 1986. It stopped 73 seconds afterward.

So did America.

During 1986, Reagan signed three major laws. The Goldwater-Nichols Act finally streamlined the U.S. military chain of command, mandating full cooperation between the various services to avoid near-fiascos like Grenada.

The Tax Reform Act flattened taxes still further, while closing loopholes and tax shelters.

I DON'T THINK THIS LAND IS WORTH ANYTHING WITHOUT A TAX SHELTER ON IT ... WHERE CAN I UNLOAD IT?

TRY A SAVINGS AND LOAN ... THEY'RE BACK ON PAGE *172.*

The Immigration Reform and Control Act stiffened the laws on undocumented workers ... but provided an amnesty (and eventual citizenship) for 2.1 million undocumented workers, mostly Mexican.

I THINK CONGRESS IS SCHIZOPHRENIC OR SOMETHING.

WELCOME TO LIFE AS AN AMERICAN, JOSE.

Congress' other occupation during 1986 was hunting down evidence of the "Iran-Contra" scandal in Reagan's National Security Council. Although the idea was to sell arms to Iran as ransom for the hostages in Lebanon, only one was freed, and Hezbollah kidnapped three more during the operation.
SO WE ASK ISRAEL TO SELL MISSILES TO IRAN FOR US, AND WE TAKE THE MONEY AND GIVE IT TO THE CONTRAS. KEEPS IT OFF THE BOOKS, NICE AND LEGAL-LIKE.
WHAT IF THEY SAY NO?
WELL, WE COULD DO IT OURSELVES, BUT WE'D HAVE TO BRING A GIFT, LIKE A CAKE OR A BIBLE.
I LOVE THIS PLAN. I'M EXCITED TO BE A PART OF IT.
All of which violated the law as well as stated administration policy on terrorism. A bipartisan commission found no proof of Reagan's direct involvement; the convictions of two NSC staffers were overturned on appeal.
A FEW MONTHS AGO, I TOLD THE AMERICAN PEOPLE I DID NOT TRADE ARMS FOR HOSTAGES. MY HEART AND MY BEST INTENTIONS STILL TELL ME THAT'S TRUE, BUT THE FACTS AND EVIDENCE TELL ME IT IS NOT.
Some people thought selling arms to Iran was sober realism compared to Reagan's 1983 Strategic Defense Initiative, a plan to build a space-based missile defense system. They called it "Star Wars," but Reagan pushed on with it, spending $27 billion on research and development.
HUNTER-KILLER SATELLITE
SOVIET ICBM
$160 BILLION?
U.S.A.
Whether or not the skeptics believed in SDI, the Soviets seemed to. The new Soviet leader, Gorbachev, cratered two summit meetings – Geneva in 1985 and Reykjavik in 1986 – by insisting that the U.S. cease SDI research.
YOU'RE NOT AS EVIL AS THE REST OF YOUR EMPIRE.
THANK YOU, ER ... I THINK.
But Gorbachev's position grew untenable. His radical perestroika policy, attempting to reform the unreformable Soviet economy, was failing. In 1987, Gorbachev and Reagan left SDI intact, but abolished intermediate-range missiles. It was the first agreement in the entire Cold War to actually reduce nuclear weapons.
IS THERE ANYTHING FURTHER, COMRADE GENERAL?
FURTHER, YOUR POLICY OF SPEAKING OPENLY IN THE SPIRIT OF GLASNOST IS A DISASTER.
In 1987, the Soviets announced they would pull out of Afghanistan. Two years later, they did.

The years ahead will be great ones for our country, for the cause of freedom and the spread of civilization. The West will not contain Communism; it will transcend Communism. We will not bother to denounce it, we'll dismiss it as a sad, bizarre chapter in human history whose last pages are even now being written."

– Ronald Reagan, May 17, 1981

Gorbachev also refused to send Soviet troops into Eastern Europe to crush protests. Poland, then Hungary, immediately elected non-Communist governments. When Hungary opened its borders in August, East Germans began to flood through them to the West. On November 9, 1989, the East German government recognized the fait accompli and opened the Berlin Wall. The unrest spread to the Soviet Union itself – it dissolved on December 26, 1991. The Cold War was over.

The president during the final Soviet collapse was Reagan's vice president, George H.W. Bush, elected by a comfortable margin in 1988.
READ MY LIPS: NO NEW TAXES.
ENVIRONMENT PRESIDENT!
A THOUSAND POINTS OF LIGHT.
THE VISION THING.
A KINDER, GENTLER AMERICA.
IT'S KIND OF HARD TO BELIEVE I'M STILL GOING TO LOSE THIS THING.
DUKAKIS FOR PRESIDENT
On March 24, 1989, the *Exxon Valdez* ran aground off Alaska and spilled 10.8 million gallons of oil in the largest oil spill in American history.
IF IT'S ANY COMFORT TO YOU, THE ENVIRONMENTAL MOVEMENT HAS BEEN REALLY ENERGIZED BY THIS WHOLE THING.
Another glitch plagued the Hubble Space Telescope, launched in 1990 with a faulty mirror. NASA eventually fixed it in 1993, opening up deep space and the distant past to observation for the first time.
35,000 anti-abortion protesters descended on Wichita, Kansas in 1991 for a "Summer of Mercy" civil disobedience campaign that ended with 2,700 arrests. In 1994, Congress made such civil disobedience tactics federal crimes.
In another echo of Sixties turmoil, Los Angeles exploded in a race riot after police brutality to a black man named Rodney King. When the six days of riots ended on May 4, 1992, 53 people were dead, including 25 blacks, 16 Hispanics, 8 whites, and 2 Asians.

But most of Bush's attention was overseas, and not just on the disintegrating Soviet empire. In December of 1989, U.S. troops invaded Panama to depose its dictator, Manuel Noriega, who took refuge in the Vatican Embassy.
I'LL COME OUT IF YOU'LL JUST PLAY SOME CLAPTON.
ROCK

In August 1990, Iraqi dictator Saddam Hussein conquered his neighbor Kuwait, eventually triggering a U.S.-led retaliatory air attack and invasion under UN auspices.
HOOAH! IT'S JUST LIKE THE KOREAN WAR ALL OVER AGAIN!
UM...

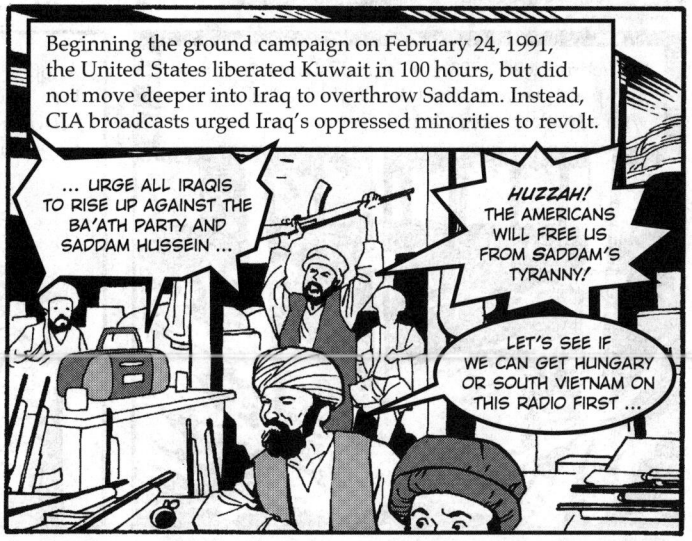
Beginning the ground campaign on February 24, 1991, the United States liberated Kuwait in 100 hours, but did not move deeper into Iraq to overthrow Saddam. Instead, CIA broadcasts urged Iraq's oppressed minorities to revolt.
... URGE ALL IRAQIS TO RISE UP AGAINST THE BA'ATH PARTY AND SADDAM HUSSEIN ...
HUZZAH! THE AMERICANS WILL FREE US FROM SADDAM'S TYRANNY!
LET'S SEE IF WE CAN GET HUNGARY OR SOUTH VIETNAM ON THIS RADIO FIRST ...

When the Kurds and Shiites did so, Saddam's forces killed tens of thousands of them. Although Bush did not intervene in the rebellion, he did eventually impose "no-fly zones" which stabilized the situation and allowed an independent Kurdish region to flourish.
TANKS ONLY, DOWN THERE! TANKS ONLY!

In December 1992, President Bush deployed American troops to safeguard a UN famine-relief mission in Somalia. On October 3, 1993, 18 American soldiers died in a massive street battle in Mogadishu; the new president withdrew American forces the next year.

Democratic Arkansas Governor Bill Clinton ran against President Bush. A brief recession, and the independent candidacy of millionaire Ross Perot, helped Clinton over the top with 43% of the vote.

Among Clinton's first acts was to sign the stalled Family Leave Act, allowing working women time off from their employers for pregnancy. Working women were increasingly likely to be employers: by 1996, American women owned 7.7 million businesses, and about 25% of corporate vice presidents were female.

On February 26, 1993, the radical Islamist terrorist group al-Qaeda attacked the World Trade Center with a truck bomb, killing six people.

Another major Clinton priority was passing the North American Free Trade Agreement, which dramatically lowered trade barriers between Mexico, Canada, and the United States and created the largest free-trade bloc in the world.

American borders opened to new immigrants as well; 1.4 million Chinese, 1.4 million Central Americans, and 1.7 million South Asians were among the 9 million legal immigrants in the 1990s.

In 1993, Clinton rammed through a combination of tax hikes and spending halts to cut the deficit. It proved unpopular in the 1994 mid-term elections.

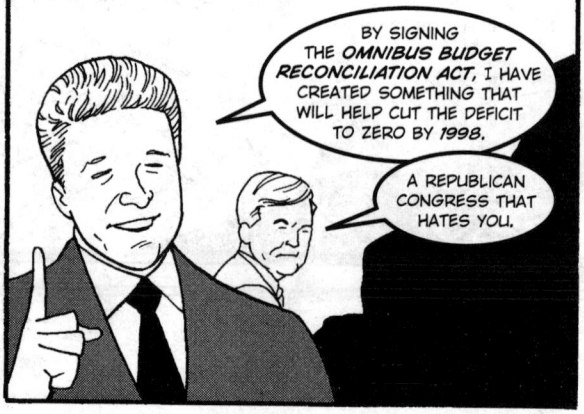

But by then the economy had come out of the 1991 recession. One impetus was the creation of the World Wide Web by a European team – and the introduction in 1993 of the first popular graphical web browser, Mosaic, by Marc Andreesen at the University of Illinois.

Once anyone could find the Web, Americans found money in it. In just five years, the Internet economy in the United States was over $300 billion, employing 1.2 million Americans. It was the economic equivalent of creating the entire U.S. automotive industry in five years, without the pollution.

YOU ORDERED A NEW ECONOMY ONLINE, RIGHT? SIGN HERE.

On April 19, 1995, a paranoid former security guard named Timothy McVeigh detonated a truck bomb at a federal office building in Oklahoma City, killing 168 people. The Clinton administration responded with a major FBI operation against right-wing "militia movements" in the U.S.

The Soviet collapse triggered a similar collapse in Yugoslavia in 1991. In 1995, the United States led NATO in a series of air strikes on Serbian forces in Bosnia to force a peace. Clinton sent U.S. troops into Bosnia after the accords as peacekeepers.

THIS CAN'T END WELL.

In 1996, Republicans in Congress and Clinton passed a welfare reform act tying welfare benefits to work. Welfare case loads dropped sharply afterward, as did child poverty.

Bill

Al-Qaeda attacked America again on August 7, 1998. Two simultaneous car bombs damaged the U.S. Embassies in Kenya and Tanzania, killing 233 people, including 12 Americans.

But more important things were happening in Washington! In 1998, President Clinton committed perjury in a sexual harassment suit, and the Republican House decided to impeach him for it. The Republican Senate voted to find him not guilty, and Clinton's job approval ratings rose despite the whole debacle.
I DID NOT HAVE SEXUAL RELATIONS WITH THAT WOMAN.
IT DEPENDS ON WHAT THE MEANING OF THE WORD "IS" ... IS.
WHAT WAS THE QUESTION AGAIN?
In 1999, the Yugoslavian war had spread into Serbia itself. Again, the United States led NATO air attacks, this time against Serbia, to safeguard the minority Muslim Kosovar population. After 80 days, the Serbs again backed down, and U.S. troops joined the UN peacekeeping force in Kosovo.
SERIOUSLY, WHAT PART OF "OVERWHELMING AIR SUPERIORITY" DO YOU PEOPLE NOT UNDERSTAND?
On October 12, 2000, al-Qaeda suicide bombers struck the USS Cole in the port of Aden, killing 17 American sailors.
67
In 2000, Clinton's vice president, Al Gore, ran against the Republican governor of Texas (and son of the previous President Bush), George W. Bush. The hard-fought election came down to Florida's electoral votes, though Gore won the popular vote.
FLORIDA
A series of recounts and lawsuits mounted up until the Supreme Court ruled 5-4 that Florida's recount was not only unconstitutional but irreparable. George W. Bush thus won the narrowest Presidential election victory in American history.
BY A VOTE OF 5-4, THIS COURT RULES THAT THE PRESIDENT-ELECT OF THE UNITED STATES IS ... SAMUEL J. TILDEN.

On September 11, 2001, al-Qaeda terrorists hijacked four U.S. airliners, piloting two into the World Trade Center and one into the Pentagon. On the fourth airliner, the passengers fought back, crashing the plane in Pennsylvania before the terrorists could destroy the U.S. Capitol Building. The attacks killed 2,974 people, and 24 remain missing.

But stiff Taliban resistance and Pashtun guerrillas kept U.S. forces from pacifying Afghanistan, or finding al-Qaeda leaders.

HEALTH SAVINGS ACCOUNTS.
PRESCRIPTION DRUG PLAN.
MM-HMM.
FINE.
NO CHILD LEFT BEHIND.
WHATEVER.
But it wasn't all foreign wars. President Bush had an ambitious domestic policy, too. It went about as well as the wars did. Initial success … then increasing resistance.
MORE REFINERIES.
FEDERAL MORTGAGE REFORM.
PRIVATIZE SOCIAL SECURITY.
IMMIGRATION AMNESTY.
NO.
NO.
NO!
HECK NO!
And what policy there was got blown away in the wind of Hurricane Katrina, which drowned New Orleans (and killed over 1,800 people) on August 29, 2005.
NOT IT!
NOT IT!
FEMA
In 2007, the sub-prime mortgage market took a hit … and in the autumn of 2008, it blew up the U.S. banking system, triggering the biggest stock-market crash since 1929.
HAVE WE LEARNED NOTHING FROM PAGE 172?
U.S. ECONOMY
Two wars, a hurricane, and a financial crisis made it the Democrats' year in 2008. Barack Obama of Chicago, only the fifth black Senator in U.S. history …
IF THERE IS ANYONE OUT THERE WHO STILL DOUBTS THAT AMERICA IS A PLACE WHERE ALL THINGS ARE POSSIBLE; WHO STILL WONDERS IF THE DREAM OF OUR FOUNDERS IS ALIVE IN OUR TIME; WHO STILL QUESTIONS THE POWER OF OUR DEMOCRACY, TONIGHT IS YOUR ANSWER.
… became the first black president in U.S. history. Maybe this can end well, after all.

Index

A

Aberdeen, Lord, 53
Abernathy, Ralph 142
Acetylene Light and Power, 101
ACT-UP, 172
Adams, John, 7, 11, 13, 27-29, 36
Adams, John Quincy, 41, 44-45
Adams, Samuel, 7, 9, 19
Adler, Dankmar, 93
Afghanistan, 184
Agnew, Spiro, 168
Aguinaldo, Emilio, 100
AIDS plague, 172
air brakes, 85
air-conditioning, 105
Alamo, siege of, 51
Alcoa, 101
Alien and Sedition Acts, 30, 36
Alien and Sedition Acts (1798), 27
Allen, Paul, 167
Altair 8800 PC, 167
Altgeld, John Peter, 92
American Federation of Labor, 91
American Indian Movement, 165
American System, 45
Andreesen, Marc, 181
Annapolis Convention, 20
Anslinger, Harry, 123
Anthony, Susan B., 80, 83
anti-abortion movement, 178
Antietam, Battle of (Civil War), 64
Apollo 11 moon landing, 164
Armour, Philip, 82
Armstrong, Louis, 120
Armstrong, Neil, 164
ARPANET, 163
Arthur, Chester A., 91
Articles of Confederation, 20-21
assembly lines, 104
Atlanta Address, 107
atomic bomb, 130
Atzerodt, George, 70

B

Baby Boom, 158
Baran, Paul, 155
Barbary War, 35-36
Barnum, P.T., 57
Barton, Clara, 91
baseball, 57
Bataan Death March (World War II), 127
Battle of Antietam (Civil War), 64
Battle of Breed's Hill (Revolutionary War), 10
Battle of Buena Vista (Mexican-American War), 54
Battle of Bunker Hill (Revolutionary War), 10
Battle of Chancellorsville (Civil War), 65
Battle of Chosin Reservoir (Korean War), 139
Battle of Concord (Revolutionary War), 10
Battle of Gettysburg (Civil War), 65-66
Battle of Lake Erie (War of 1812), 40
Battle of Leyte Gulf (World War II), 129
Battle of Little Bighorn, 87
Battle of Manassas (Civil War), 62
Battle of Mechanicsville (Civil War), 62
Battle of Midway (World War II), 127
Battle of New Orleans (War of 1812), 41
Battle of Saratoga (Revolutionary War), 14
Battle of Shiloh (Civil War), 64
Battle of the Bulge (World War II), 129
Battle of the Coral Sea (World War II), 127
Battle of Trenton (Revolutionary War), 14
Battle of Vicksburg (Civil War), 65
Battle of Yorktown (Revolutionary War), 16-17
Bay of Pigs, 154
Bear Flag Revolt, 54
Beat Generation, 150
Begin, Menachem, 169
Beirut Embassy bombing, 174
Berkman, Alexander, 95
Berlin Wall, 154
Bill of Rights, 24
bin Laden, Osama, 184
birth control pill, 158
Birth of a Nation, 106
Black Codes, 77
Black Thursday, 121

Bleeding Kansas, 59
blues music, 106
Boone, Daniel, 15
Booth, John Wilkes, 70
Borlaug, Norman, 154
Boston Massacre, 7
Boston Tea Party, 7-8
Bowie, Jim, 51
Breed's Hill, Battle of (Revolutionary War), 10
Brezhnev, Leonid, 170
Brook Farm commune, 46
Brown, John, 59
Brown v. Board of Education, 141
Bryan, William Jennings, 97, 108, 118
Buchanan, James, 59, 92
Buck v. Bell, 108
Buena Vista, Battle of (Mexican-American War), 54
Bulge, Battle of the (World War II), 129
Bunker Hill, Battle of (Revolutionary War), 10
Burgoyne, John, 14
Burnham, Daniel, 93
Burr, Aaron, 28-29, 33
Bush, George H.W., 178-180
Bush, George W., 182

C

Cable Act of 1984, 173
cable TV, 173
Calhoun, John C., 45, 47
California Gold Rush, 55-56
Cambodian invasion, Vietnam War, 165
Capone, Al, 116
Carleton, Guy, 18
Carlson, Charles, 135
Carnegie, Andrew, 81
Carnegie Steel, 81
Carpentier, Georges, 120
Carrier, Willis Haviland, 105
Carter, Jimmy, 169-170
Castro, Fidel, 152
CCC work relief program, 123
cell phones, 173
Centennial Exhibition (1876), 85
Central Park, New York City, 93
Challenger space shuttle, 175
Chancellorsville, Battle of (Civil War), 65
Chavez, Cesar, 161
Chicago Board of Trade, 82
China Trade, 46
Chinese Exclusion movement, 90
Chisholm Trail, 74
Chosin Reservoir, Battle of (Korean War), 139
Churchill, Winston, 130, 136
Civil Rights Act of 1964, 146, 157
Civil War, 60-61
  Battle of Antietam, 64
  Battle of Chancellorsville, 65
  Battle of Gettysburg, 65-66
  Battle of Manassas, 62
  Battle of Mechanicsville, 62
  Battle of Shiloh, 64
  Battle of Vicksburg, 65
  Confederate States of America, 60
  Emancipation Proclamation, 67
  March to the Sea, 69
  siege on Fort Sumter, 60
  trench warfare, 67
Clark, William, 32-33
Clay, Henry, 45, 47, 52-53, 58
Clemenceau, Georges, 115
Cleveland, Grover, 92, 96
Clinton, Bill, 180-182
Coca-Cola, 94
Cody, "Buffalo Bill," 75
Cold War, 138, 177
Colt, Samuel, 50
Colt 1836 revolver, 50
Coltrane, John, 150
Columbia space shuttle, 173
Comic Books, Golden Age, 124
comic strips, 105
Common Sense, 12
Concord, Battle of (Revolutionary War), 10
Confederate States of America, 60
Connor, Bull, 144
Constitution, 22-24
  Eighteenth Amendment, 116
  Fifteenth Amendment, 79
  Fourteenth Amendment, 78
  Thirteenth Amendment, 76
  Twelfth Amendment, 28
  Twenty-first Amendment, 123
  Twenty-fourth Amendment, 146
  Twenty-sixth Amendment, 158
Coolidge, Calvin, 118, 121
Cooper, James Fenimore, 49
Cooper, Martin, 173
Copland, Aaron, 120
Coplon, Judith, 138
Coral Sea, Battle of (World War II), 127
Cornwallis, Charles, 14, 16

counterculture movement, 158
Crash of 1873, 87
Crazy Horse, 87
Crockett, Davy, 50-51
Crook, George, 87
crossing of the Delaware River, 14
Cuban Missile Crisis, 155
Custer, George Armstrong, 87, 89
Czolgosz, Leon, 101

D

D-Day (World War II), 129
Daley, Richard J., 153
Damadian, Raymond, 173
Davis, Jefferson, 60, 78
Davis, Miles, 150
de Tocqueville, Alexis, 47
Debs, Eugene V., 97, 111, 117
Decatur, Stephen, 35
Declaration of Independence, 13
"Declaration of Sentiments," 58
Deere, John, 50
Democratic National Convention of 1968 riots, 161
Dempsey, Jack, 120
Dewey, George, 100
Dewey, John, 108
Dewey, Thomas, 137
Diem, Ngo Dihn, 156
Diners Club charge cards, 135
Dinwiddie, Robert, 5
Disney, Walt, 148
Doors, The, 158
Dos Passos, John, 119
Douglass, Frederick, 48, 80, 83, 147
Douglas, Stephen, 58-60
Dragnet, 150
Dred Scott v. Sanford, 59
DuBois, W.E.B., 107
Dukakis, Michael, 178
Dylan, Bob, 158

E

Edison, Thomas Alva, 84-85, 105, 135
Eighteenth Amendment, 116
Einstein, Albert, 130
Eisenhower, Dwight D., 127, 129, 140-142, 148-150, 152, 163
Electoral College, 25
Eliot, T.S., 119
Ellsberg, Daniel, 165
Emancipation Proclamation, 64, 67
Embargo Acts, 36
Emerson, Ralph Waldo, 57
Emperor Hirohito of Japan, 131
EPA, 163
Equal Rights Amendment, 172
Erie Canal, 45
Espionage and Sedition Acts of 1918, 111
eugenics, 108
Exclusion Treaty of 1880, 90
Exxon Valdez, 178

F

Family Leave Act, 180
Federal Reserve Act, 110
Federalist Papers, 24
Federation of Organized Trades and Labor Unions, 91
Fifteenth Amendment, 79
Fifty-Four Forty or Fight, 53
Fillmore, Millard, 59
First Continental Congress, 8
First Great Awakening, 37
Fisk, Jim, 81
Flatiron Building, 93
Florida election recount, 182
flu epidemic of 1918, 114
fluoroscope, 84
football, 79
Ford, Gerald, 168-169
Ford, Henry, 104
Ford, John, 150
Fort Sumter, 60
Foster, Stephen, 57
Fourteen Points, 115
Fourteenth Amendment, 78
Franklin, Benjamin, 6-7, 12-13, 18, 22-23, 84
Freedmen's Bureau, 77
Freedom Rides, 143
Fremont, John C., 54
French and Indian War, 5-6
Frick, Henry Clay, 95
Fugitive Slave Act of 1850, 58
Fulton, Robert, 36

G

Gagarin, Yuri, 153
Gall, 87
Gallatin, Albert, 30, 36
Garfield, James A., 83, 91
Garrison, William Lloyd, 48, 58
Gates, Bill, 167
GATT (General Agreement on Tariffs and Trade), 136
gay liberation movement, 163
Gay Men's Health Crisis, 172
General Agreement on Tariffs and Trade (GATT), 136
Geronimo, 88, 90

Gershwin, George, 120
Gettysburg, Battle of (Civil War), 65-66
Gettysburg Address, 66
Ghost Dance movement, 88
GI Bill of 1944, 134
Gilded Age, 81
Gold Rush, 55-56, 87
Goldwater, Barry, 156
Goldwater-Nichols Act of 1986, 175
Goliad Massacre (Texas Revolution), 51
Gompers, Samuel, 91
Gorbachev, Mikhail, 176-177
Gore, Al, 182
Gould, Jay, 81
Graham, Sylvester, 46
Grant, Ulysses S., 63-65, 68-69, 79, 83
Great Depression, 121-124
Great Fire of Chicago, 82
Great Migration, 114, 127
Great Society, 157
Green Revolution, 154
Greene, Nathanael, 16
Grenada, invasion, 174
Griffith, D.W., 105
Gulf War, 179

H

Haloid Company, 101
Hamilton, Alexander, 20-21, 24-25, 28, 33
Hancock, John, 7, 9, 11, 13, 19
Handy, W.C., 106
Harding, Warren G., 117
Harrison, Benjamin, 95-96
Harrison, William Henry, 38, 52
Hart-Celler Act of 1965, 157
Hawaii, 97
Hawthorne, Nathaniel, 57
Hayes, Rutherford B., 86, 89, 90
Haymarket Square, bombing, 92
Hearst, William Randolph, 94
Henry, Patrick, 12, 23-24
Hezbollah, 174
Hiawatha, 57
hippie movement, 158
Hiroshima, 131
Hiss, Alger, 138
Hitler, Adolf, 125-126
HMS Leopard, 36
Ho Chi Minh Trail (Vietnam War), 159
Home Insurance Building, 93
homelessness crisis, 172
Homestead Act, 74
Homestead Strike, 95
Hoover, Herbert, 121-122
Hoover, J. Edgar, 142
Housing Act of 1949, 149
Howe, William, 10
Hubble Space Telescope, 178
Huckleberry Finn, 94
Humphrey, Hubert, 161
Hurricane Katrina, 185
Hussein, Suddam, 179, 184
hydrogen bomb, 151

I

I Love Lucy, 150
IBM, 101
Immigration Reform and Control Act of 1986, 175
incandescent lamp, 84
Independence Hall, 21-22
Indian Removal Act of 1830, 49
industrial research laboratories, 84
integrated circuits, 153
International Red Cross, 91
International Time Recording Company, 101
Intolerable Acts of 1774, 8
Iran Hostage Crisis, 170
Iran-Contra scandal, 174-176
Iraq War, 184-185

J

Jackson, Andrew, 41, 44-45, 47, 49, 52, 110
Jackson, Thomas J., 61-62, 65
Jay, John, 24, 26
jazz, 105
Jazz Age, 120
Jefferson, Thomas, 13, 20, 25, 27-28, 30, 33-36
Jenney, William LeBaron, 93
Jim Crow Laws, 106
Jobs, Steve, 167
Johnson, Andrew, 70, 76-78
Johnson, Lyndon, 146, 153, 156-157, 159, 162
Joseph, Chief, 87
judicial review, 29
Judiciary Act of 1789, 29

K

Kaiser, Henry J., 128
Kansas-Nebraska Act of 1854, 59
Kearney, Dennis, 90
Kennedy, John F., 144, 146, 153-155, 161
Kennedy, Robert F., 144, 161
Kent State shooting, 165
Khrushchev, Nikita, 151-152, 155

Kilby, Jack, 153
Kim Il-Sung, 139
King Jr., Martin Luther, 142, 144-145, 161
King, Rodney, 178
King Charles IV of Spain, 31
King George III, 7, 13, 18
Kissinger, Henry, 162
Knights of Labor, 91
Korean War, 139-141
  Battle of Chosin Reservoir, 139
Ku Klux Klan, 78

L

Lafayette, Marquis de, 16
Lalawethika, 37
Last of the Mohicans, The, 49
Lauterbur, Paul, 173
Leaves of Grass, 57
Lee, Richard Henry, 12
Lee, Robert E., 59, 61, 64-65, 68
Lend-Lease, 125
Lewis, John, 143, 146
Lewis, John L., 124
Lewis, Meriwether, 32-33
Leyte Gulf, Battle of (World War II), 129
Liberator newspaper, 48
Lincoln, Abraham, 54, 59-61, 64, 66-68, 70
Lindbergh, Charles, 119, 125
Little Bighorn, Battle of, 87
Lost Generation, 119
Louis XVI, 14
Louisiana Purchase, 31, 33
lynchings, 106

M

MacArthur, Douglas, 129, 139-140
Madison, James, 20-24, 29, 36
magnetic tape, 135
Maiman, Theodore H., 153
Manassas, Battle of (Civil War), 62
Manhattan Project, 130
maps
  North America (1754), 5
  Transcontinental Railroad, 75
  Ulysses S. Grant Civil War campaigns, 68
  United States (1804), 33
  United States (1820), 45
  United States (1860), 60
Marbury, William, 29
Marbury v. Madison, 29
March to the Sea (Civil War), 69
Marshall, George C., 128, 136, 148
Marshall, John, 29, 33, 45, 49
Marshall Plan, 136
Marx, Karl, 90
McCarthy, Joseph, 138, 148
McClellan, George, 62, 64, 67-68
McCormick, Cyrus, 50
McCulloch v. Maryland, 45
McDowell, Irving, 61
McGovern, George, 166, 168
McKay, Winsor, 105
McKinley, William, 97, 100-101
McNamara, Robert, 159-160
McVeigh, Timothy, 181
mechanical reaper, 50
Mechanicsville, Battle of (Civil War), 62
Melville, Herman, 57
Mencken, H.L., 117-118
Mexican-American War, 53-54
  Battle of Buena Vista, 54
  Bear Flag Revolt, 54
microwave oven, 135
Midway, Battle of (World War II), 127
Miles, Nelson, 87-88
militia movement, 181
Miller, William, 46
mimeograph, 84
Missouri Compromise, 59
Moby-Dick, 57
Model T, 104
Monroe, James, 31, 44
Monroe Doctrine, 44
Moody, Dwight, 96
Morgan, J.P., 81, 83, 97
Morris, Gouverneur, 21
Morse, Samuel, 52
Morton, Jelly Roll, 105
motion picture industry, 105
Mott, Lucretia, 58
Mount Vernon, 20

N

NAACP (National Association for the Advancement of Colored People), 107
NAFTA (North American Free Trade Agreement), 180
Nagasaki, 131
Napoleon Boneparte, 31, 41
National Broadcasting Company, 120
National Interstate and Defense Highways Act of 1956, 149
NATO (North Atlantic Treaty Organization), 138
Neutrality Act of 1935, 125
New Deal, 123
New Orleans, Battle of (War of 1812), 41
Niagara Falls, 101
Nimitz, Chester, 127

Nixon, Richard, 153, 162-163, 165-166, 168, 170, 172
Noriega, Manuel, 179
North River Steamboat, 36

O

Obama, Barack, 185
Office of the Budget, 117
Ohio, 31
Olmstead, Frederick Law, 93
OPEC oil embargo, 166
Osceola, 48-49
OSHA, 163
Oswald, Lee Harvey, 156

P–Q

Pacific Railway Act of 1862, 75
Paine, Thomas, 12
Palmer, Mitchell, 114-115
Panama Canal, 102
Panic of 1873, 83-84, 89-90
Parks, Rosa, 141, 146
Patton, George S., 113, 129
Peace Corps, 154
Pearl Harbor, attack, 126
Pendleton Act of 1881, 91
Pentagon Papers, 165
perestroika, 176
Perot, Ross, 180
Perry, Oliver Hazard, 40
Pershing, John J., 112
Personal Responsibility and Work Opportunity Act, 181
phonograph, 84
Pierce, Franklin, 59
Pitcairn, John, 3
Pittsburgh Reduction Company, 101
Plan of Chicago, 1909, 93
Plessy v. Ferguson, 106
Polk, James K., 53-54
popular sovereignty, 59
Populist Party, 96
Potsdam Conference (World War II), 136
Powell, Lewis, 70
Powers, Francis Gary, 152
Prohibition, 116
Prosser, Gabriel, 34
Pulitzer, Joseph, 94
Pullman Sleeping Car Company strike, 96-97

R

Randolph, A. Philip, 144
Raven and Other Poems, The, 57
RCA, 120
Reagan, Nancy, 172
Reagan, Ronald, 161, 163, 171-172, 174, 176
Reconstruction, 77-78
recreational drug use, 158
Revels, Hiram, 78
Revere, Paul, 7, 9
Revival Movement, 37
Revolutionary War, 9, 11-12
  Battle of Breed's Hill, 10
  Battle of Bunker Hill, 10
  Battle of Concord, 10
  Battle of Saratoga, 14
  Battle of Trenton, 14
  Battle of Yorktown, 16-17
  Boston Massacre, 7
  Boston Tea Party, 7-8
  crossing of the Delaware River, 14
  Declaration of Independence, 13
  Intolerable Acts of 1774, 8
  shot heard 'round the world, 3-4
  Stamp Act of 1776, 6-7
  Treaty of 1783, 18
"Rhapsody in Blue," 120
Roberts, Edward, 167
Robinson, Jackie, 137
Rockefeller, John D., 81, 104, 109-110
Roe v. Wade, 166
Rogers, Will, 117
Rommel, Erwin, 128
Roosevelt Corollary, 101
Roosevelt, Franklin D., 123-126, 130
Roosevelt, Theodore, 100-102, 108-109
Rosie the Riveter, 128
Rustin, Bayard, 142

S

Sadat, Anwar, 169
Salk, Jonas, 148
SALT II arms limitation treaty of 1979, 170
San Francisco Earthquake, 102
Santa Anna, 50-51, 54
Saratoga, Battle of (Revolutionary War), 14
Sarnoff, David, 120, 147
savings and loan crisis, 172
Scarlet Letter, The, 57
Schmitt, Harrison, 164
Schulz, Charles M., 148
scientific management, 108
Scopes, John D., 118
Scott, Winfield, 54
SDI X-ray laser satellite, 176
Sears, Roebuck & Company, 94
SEATO Treaty, 156
Second Continental Congress, 11, 13
Second Great Awakening, 37, 46-47
Seguin, Juan, 51

Selective Service Act of 1917, 111
Seminole Wars, 48-49
Seward, William H., 70
sharecropping, 77
Shays, Daniel, 19
Sherman, William Tecumseh, 68-69, 77
Sherman Anti-Trust Act of 1890, 95
Shiloh, Battle of (Civil War), 64
Sholes and Glidden Remington typewriter, 85
shot heard 'round the world, 3-4
Shuttlesworth, Fred, 143
silicon chip, 153
Sirhan, Sirhan, 161
Sitting Bull, 87
slave trade, 34
Smith, Joseph, 46
Smoot-Hawley tariff of 1930, 122
Social Security, 124
sod-busting, 50
South Dakota Gold Rush, 87
Spanish flu, 114
Spanish-American War, 100
Spirit of '76, 18
Sputnik, 152
Square Deal, 101
Stalin, Joseph, 129-130, 136, 139, 151
Stamp Act of 1765, 6-7
Standard Oil, 81, 109
Stanton, Elizabeth Cady, 58, 80
Statue of Liberty, 85
Stowe, Harriet Beecher, 58
Strategic Defense Initiative of 1983, 176
Strauss, Levi, 56
Strike of 1877, 89-90
sub-prime mortgage crisis, 185
suburban development, 149
Sullivan, John, 15
Sullivan, Louis, 93
Summer of Love (1967), 158
Swift, Gustavus, 82

T

Taft, William Howard, 100, 108-109, 117
Taft-Hartley Act of 1947, 134
Taney, Roger, 52, 59
Tax Reform Act of 1986, 175
Taylor, Frederick Winslow, 108
Taylor, Zachary, 54, 59
Tecumseh, 37-38
telegraph, 52
Tennessee Valley Authority, 123
Tenskwatawa, 37-38
Tesla, Nikola, 101
Tet Offensive (Vietnam War), 160
Texas Revolution, 50-51
  Goliad Massacre, 51
  siege of Alamo, 51
Thieu, Nguyen Van, 162
Third Great Awakening, 96
Thirteenth Amendment, 76
Thoreau, Henry David, 142
Tilden, Samuel, 86
Till, Emmett, 141
Torrio, Johnny, 116
Trail of Tears, 49
trail to the Great Salt Lake, 55
Transcontinental Railroad, 75
transistors, 135
Treaty of Ghent (War of 1812), 41
Treaty of Paris (1783), 18
Treaty of Versailles, (World War I), 115
trench warfare, 67
Trenton, Battle of (Revolutionary War), 14
trickle-down economics, 172
Truman, Harry S, 130, 134, 136-138, 140
Tubman, Harriet, 58
Turner, Frederick Jackson, 50
Turner, Nat, 48
Twain, Mark, 94, 100
Tweed, William M., 86
Twelfth Amendment, 28
Twenty-first Amendment, 123
Twenty-fourth Amendment, 146
Twenty-sixth Amendment, 158
Twilight Zone, The, 150
Tyler, John, 52

U

U-2 spy planes, 152
Uncas, 49
Uncle Tom's Cabin, 58
Union Carbide, 101
USS Chesapeake, 36

V

Van Buren, Martin, 47, 52, 96
Veterans' Bureau, 117
Vicksburg, Battle of (Civil War), 65
Vietnam War, 156, 159, 165
  beginning, 154
  Cambodian invasion, 165
  ending, 166
  escalation, 159
  Ho Chi Minh Trail, 159

Tet Offensive, 160
Vietnamization, 162
Villa, Pancho, 110
VisiCalc spreadsheet software, 173
V-J Day (World War II), 134
Volcker, Paul, 171-172
Voting Rights Act of 1965, 146

W

Wagner Act of 1935, 124
Wainwright Building, 93
Walden, 57
Wallace, George, 146, 162
Wallace, Lew, 64
War of 1812, 38-39, 41
Battle of Lake Erie, 40
Battle of New Orleans, 41
Treaty of Ghent, 41
war on drugs, 172
Warren, Earl, 127
Washington, Booker T., 107
Washington, George, 5, 11, 15, 18, 20-22, 25, 44
Watergate Scandal, 168
Webster, Daniel, 45
Welfare Reform Act of 1996, 181
Westinghouse, George, 85, 101
Westmoreland, William, 160
Whiskey Rebellion, 26
White, Harry Dexter, 138
White City, 93
Whitney, Eli, 25
Wilson, Woodrow, 109-110, 115
Women's Liberation movement, 163
Woodhull, Victoria, 83
Woodstock Music Festival, 158
Worcester v. Georgia, 49
Workingmen's Party, 90
World Trade Center (1993), 180
World Trade Center (2001), 183
World War I, 112-115
Treaty of Versailles, 115
World War II, 125-131, 134
Bataan Death March, 127
Battle of Leyte Gulf, 129
Battle of the Bulge, 129
Battle of the Coral Sea, 127
Battle of the Midway, 127
D-Day, 129
Hiroshima bombing, 131
Nagasaki bombing, 131
Pearl Harbor attack, 126
Potsdam Conference, 136
V-J Day, 134
Yalta Conference, 130
Wounded Knee Creek, 88
Wovoka, 88
Wozniak, Steve, 167
Wright, Frank Lloyd, 102
Wright, Orville, 103-104
Wright, Wilbur, 103-104

X-Y-Z

xerography, 135
Xerox, 101
X, Malcolm, 150, 159

Yalta Coference (World War II), 130
Yorktown, Battle of (Revolutionary War), 16-17
Young, Brigham, 55

Zoot Suit Riots, 127
Zworykin, Vladimir, 147

Check out these BEST-SELLERS

READ BY MILLIONS!

978-1-59257-115-4
$16.95

978-1-59257-458-2
$19.95

978-1-59257-566-4
$22.95

978-1-59257-485-8
$24.95

978-1-59257-480-3
$19.95

978-1-59257-469-8
$14.95

978-1-59257-439-1
$18.95

978-1-59257-483-4
$14.95

978-1-59257-389-9
$18.95

978-1-59257-471-1
$18.95

978-1-59257-437-7
$19.95

978-1-59257-463-6
$14.95

978-0-02864244-4
$21.95

978-1-59257-335-6
$19.95

978-1-59257-491-9
$19.95

More than **450 titles** available at booksellers and online retailers everywhere

ALPHA

www.idiotsguides.com

Let history be your guide!

978-1-59257-869-6

New in June 2009!

978-1-59257-853-5

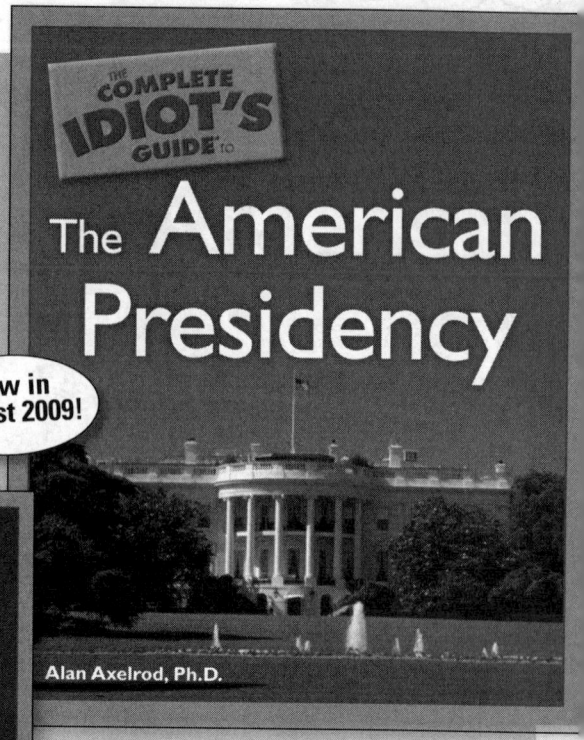

New in August 2009!

978-1-59257-912-9

978-1-59257-831-3

978-1-59257-791-0

978-1-59257-627-2

978-1-59257-712-5

978-1-59257-489-6

Check out twenty other history titles in *The Complete Idiot's Guide®* series.

ALPHA

idiotsguides.com